22024473973

D0528317

THE BUSINESS OF
W·O·M·E·N·S
MAGAZINES

JOAN BARRELL
◆
BRIAN BRAITHWAITE

RIDING HOUSE STREET LIBRARY, PCL
37-49 RIDING HOUSE STREET, W1P 7PT

**KOGAN
PAGE**

First published in 1979 by Associated Business Press
This edition first published in 1988
by Kogan Page Ltd, 120 Pentonville Road
London N1 9JN

© Brian Braithwaite and Joan Barrell 1988

British Library Cataloguing in Publication Data
Braithwaite, Brian
    The business of women's magazines. — 2nd ed
    1. Women's serials in English. Serials
    with British imprints, to 1987
    I. Title   II. Barrell, Joan
    052

    ISBN 1-85091-627-6

All rights reserved. No part of this publication
may be reproduced, stored in a retrieval system, or
transmitted in any form or by any means, electronic,
mechanical, photocopying, recording or otherwise,
without the prior permission in writing of the publishers

Printed in Great Britain

CONTENTS

ACKNOWLEDGEMENTS

We would like to thank the following for their help in various ways in assisting us in putting together this book: Catherine Whitehead, Brian Boddy, David Hepworth, Linda Kelsey, Deirdre McSharry, Judith Hall, Jill Churchill, Sue Dobson, Sue James, Annette Lillis and Simon Braithwaite.

The authors would like to point out that the views expressed in the book are their own and not necessarily those of the National Magazine Company, of which they are both directors.

PREFACE

We published our book *The Business of Women's Magazines* in 1978. By comparison with today the women's magazine scene was tranquil. We had seen the turbulence caused by the launching of *Cosmopolitan* in 1972, the ripples from the launch still drifting across the magazine pond. By the time *Company* was launched in 1978, there had been a plethora of births and deaths and a couple of still-births. But, as a whole, the scene was one of fairly normal commercial life – win a few, lose a few.

In our book we took a historical aspect and examined in particular the 1950s and the 1960s. We have left these chapters reasonably intact in this new edition, with some amendments and corrections. We found that the post-war history of women's magazines held a fascination for both catchments of readers. The more greying of our readers enjoyed the reminiscent recollections of magazines gone by – magazines they had read, or bought space in or worked on. Our younger readers, the post-war 'Baby boomers', were intrigued by the catalogue of titles which came and went or survived. After all, it is a surprising 23 years since the launch of *Nova* by Newnes: the word 'rattle' would have had a different connotation at that time to a few of the contemporary media tigers. Similarly, we have retained the record of the activities of the 1970s and examine what has happened since 1978.

We have extended and modernised our section on launches – successful or otherwise. Hindsight gives us the advantage of sagacity, but we have also endeavoured to examine and analyse the reasons for success or failure. The sackful of cuttings which we have kept over the last decade have been particularly intriguing in studying the optimistic hopes and dreams of new entrants into our overcrowded and intensely competitive market. Companies, personnel and titles have come and gone – it is a fast-moving, volatile stage on which we magazine publishers play out our dramas, thrillers and, sometimes, farces. It is a business redolent with the courageous, if sometimes foolhardy, tycoons and innovators who are convinced that there is always room on the news-shelves for one more title.

As we have been assembling this book the magazine business has been experiencing a maelstrom. New titles have been springing up like mushrooms on a compost heap. Domestic publishers, continental publishers, American publishers – the great discovery of 1987 was the hitherto rather static British women's market. The astounding success of *Prima* has opened a flood-gate. The new buzz-phrase is 'global publishing'. Like so many 'new' concepts global publishing has been around a long time – Time-Life, Reader's Digest, Condé Nast and the Hearst Corporation have all, in their own corporate styles, exploited the opportunities offered by international publishing. But all the subsequent activity, and counter-activity, occasioned by the new wave of innovative energy has created a new ball-game. We like to think that it is more important than ever that a book such as this needs to be written, to record and interpret the shifting sands of our business.

We have, of course, kept the most popular feature of our original book – the considerably expanded magazine biography, or bibliography, which represents the only attempt to marshall together the births, marriages and deaths of most of the important women's magazines published since the end of the First World War.

1

IN THE BEGINNING

The history of women's magazines begins rather improbably in the late seventeenth century. Cynthia White, in her admirably researched book, *Women's Magazines 1693–1968*, which has become a definitive work, records the first title as *The Ladies' Mercury* and dates it 1693. *The Tatler* was launched, full of tittle-tattle from the coffee houses, in 1709. Its two year publishing break in the 1960s cannot take away its impressive standing as Britain's oldest living magazine. The 1770s saw a crop of almanacs, or diaries, especially aimed at women. These were largely social and domestic chronologies with a smattering of instruction on etiquette and social manners. Towards the end of the century emerged the beginnings of the women's periodical press with the advent of *The Lady's Magazine*. This was intended to be fairly egalitarian in its readership and offered a varied editorial diet of both instruction and entertainment.

Twenty years later saw the appearance of *The Lady's Monthly Museum* which, although emphasising domestic duty, ventured into a wide sphere of education as well as society fashion. *La Belle Assemblée* was published in 1806, with much the same formula as its rivals. Letters to the editor were becoming a popular feature of the magazines – a welcome safety-valve perhaps for the repressed or depressed young lady who could anonymously consult the experts on her social, domestic or matrimonial problems.

In the 1830s these three magazines, although published separately, were welded into a publishing unit. This was the forerunner of the 'merger', a word which will appear many times in this book. The merger of magazines seems as natural and inevitable to the human condition as the merging of bodies in holy matrimony – often with the same disastrous results. In 1847 the three titles ceased publication altogether, thus starting a process which would be emulated for a hundred years.

The Victorian era arrived with its noble illusions of Woman. The 'little woman', the 'ball and chain', the 'better half' was the role expected of the lady of the house. Home and children were the extent of her working life, coupled with the busy social and travelling whirl in which the better-off Victorians enjoyed their prosperous world. Victoria was on the throne, Britannia ruled the waves, half the world was coloured red on the nursery atlas and the working class knew their place. It was only natural that the new emerging women's magazines would reflect this smug and comfortable world. New titles began to appear: *The New Monthly Belle Assemblée*, *The Englishwoman's Magazine*, *The Female's Friend*, *The Ladies' Cabinet*, *The Ladies' Journal*, *Mother's Friend*, *Lady's Review* and many others. The market became almost as crowded as it is today; the Victorian lady could take her choice as she was regaled with news and notes on cookery and fashion, dressmaking and etiquette, literary criticism and gardening.

It is interesting to note that the cover price of women's magazines was very high. The usual price was a shilling, which was a considerable sum by current value – the equivalent of today's £1. Of course, for the first part of the century women's magazines were projected to the upper class who could afford the odd shilling for their entertainment.

Books were also expensive at this time, hence the popularity of the fictional part-works written by Charles Dickens and others. A series of taxes helped to keep up the costs of reading matter but these were soon abolished. The advertising tax was abolished in 1853, stamp duty in 1855 and paper duty in 1861. The way was open for cheaper and less sophisticated publications which all had a family appeal and on average cost 2d. Typical were *Dickens' Household Words*, *Mirror of Literature, Amusement and Instruction* and *The Family Friend*, which began life as a monthly and became weekly via fortnightly publications. In 1842 Mr Mudie established his lending library in Oxford Street and H Smith started to build up his chain of bookstalls, closely allied to the startling advance of the railway system. The first W H Smith railway bookstall opened on Euston Station on 1 November 1848. There were to be disputes with the railway companies in 1905 but by the following year W H Smith had established 144 shops on stations or station approaches.

Mr Mudie's Circulating Library was flourishing in the middle of the century. Based originally in Upper King Street (now Southampton Row) the business was moved in the 1850s to New Oxford Street. Mudie's operated on an unprecedented scale, exercising great influence on the popular literature of the day. It was his practice to place large advance orders for books of which he approved. He also ran famous literary reunions in the hall of the New Oxford Street headquarters which prominent literary figures would attend. When Mudie's finally went into liquidation in 1936 there were 140 branches. There is no doubt that Mudie's was a considerable factor in developing the public taste for reading.

W H Smith had begun in 1792, based on the distribution of newspapers, magazines and other periodicals. By 1855 it had already become the largest wholesale and retail news agency in England and Wales. They also began their famous library in 1858, far exceeding the horizons of Mr Mudie because of their country-wide network of railway bookstalls. The 1830s saw the beginnings of another historic bookshop chain when John Menzies set up in business as a retail bookseller in Princes Street, Edinburgh. He was soon to expand into the wholesale trade and the handling of newspapers and periodicals. He ventured into publishing on his own account with Scottish guide books and a famous work on the costumes of the clans. In 1857 he linked up with the Scottish Central Railway by taking the railway bookstalls at Perth, Stirling and Bridge of Allan. The network rapidly expanded. The first women's magazine handled by Menzies was the *People's Friend*, published in 1869 by the Thomson family at Dundee. There can be little doubt that the rapid and comprehensive build-up of the railway bookstall networks must have been of considerable importance to the development of the popular women's magazines of the time.

However, in 1852 the first of the magazine whizzkids appeared on the scene. The 21-year-old Samuel Beeton, who can only be rated as a publishing genius, produced his first enterprise, *The Englishwoman's Domestic Magazine*. This was published monthly at the sensationally low price of 2d. Mr Beeton's startling venture opened up the market to the vast middle-class market. Here was a massive new audience, hitherto excluded from the luxury of a quality monthly magazine, who for 2d could now be kept abreast of the latest developments in fashion and dressmaking as well as serialised fiction and all the other 'departments' that the modern magazine enjoys. And for an added bonus they could digest the culinary skills of the proprietor's wife, one Isabella Beeton. Mr Beeton was rewarded with an instant success, seeing his magazine attain a circulation of up to 50,000 within a few years.

There was also a gleam of women's rights appearing on the market. Magazines like *The Female's Friend* (1846) appeared briefly on the scene but the general pattern of women's magazines in the Victorian era was domestic and the several attempts at women's liberation, even in the mildest forms, were commercially unsuccessful. The 'Women's Movement' was as unpopular with the vast majority of Victorian women as it was condemned by their menfolk. Hence the steady advance of women's magazines that knew their place, just as their readers were expected to know *their* place.

Mr Beeton, never a man to stand still, followed his earlier success by launching *The Queen* in 1861, Queen Victoria giving her gracious permission for the use of the name. The cover price was 6d and the masthead was grandly decorated with a drawing of Windsor Castle. The audience was admirably defined – here was a magazine for the rich and leisured woman. *The Queen* reflected her life as she moved in the top social circles. It reflected her clothes, her life-style, her travels, and the whole society scene as it affected the *Queen* reader. Mr Beeton had scored a bull's-eye again and his new title was to survive for over a hundred years.

There was considerable expansion of the market during the last quarter of the century. With the 1870 Education Act the ball of elementary education started rolling, and later acts extended the scope of education to all classes. Here was the magazine and newspaper fodder that was to revolutionise the industry. The great burst of magazines on to the market exploited this new reading public and the rapid growth of the railway – which speeded distribution – coupled with the technical changes in printing machinery, altered the entire shape and scope of the market. New publishing giants emerged on the scene. Alfred Harmsworth, George Newnes and Arthur Pearson were names that were not only to pioneer the mass industry but to echo through the corridors of the publishing industry for many decades to come. The railways, of course, also generated a new class of traveller who bought magazines to while away the time on their journeys.

Alfred Harmsworth had started writing at school by editing the Henley House School Magazine. He became assistant editor on *Youth* and then wrote social paragraphs for *Vanity Fair* and stories for a boys' paper called *Young Folks*. He sold articles to *Titbits* (owned and edited by George Newnes) and there met Arthur Pearson who was destined to become his greatest rival. In June 1888 Harmsworth founded the weekly publication *Answers to Correspondents* which was later shortened to *Answers* and was taken over by his brother Harold in 1889. Harmsworth's empire eventually numbered more than 70 weekly and monthly publications. A vital part of his success was his insight into what working people wanted to read and his recognition of their need for some form of cut-out from their drab lives. He gave them romance, excitement and entertainment through his papers long before the glamour of the cinema arrived. Both Harmsworth and Pearson produced bright new weeklies planned for 'down market'. There was also the very popular *Family Herald Supplement* (which contained weekly serials about the 'high life' – i.e. above stairs), a monthly for the more educated called *The Strand*, and *The Idler* edited by Jerome K Jerome of *Three Men in a Boat* fame. By 1889 the youth of Britain was regaled with a penny illustrated weekly called *Ally Sloper's Half Holiday*, the halfpenny *Comic Cuts* and *Forget Me Not* for girls.

Then a problem appeared on the horizon which is still very much with us today. As the circulation of the women's magazines grew so did the costs of printing, paper and distribution. The cover prices did not cover these costs any more than they do today, so the Victorian publisher was forced to turn to the advertiser to subsidise his publication and to provide him with a profit. The advertising business was just emerging, as was the advertising agent. Despite inherent editorial disapproval of the advertiser, the revoking of the advertising tax earlier in the century unleashed a new force that was to be the life-blood of the magazine industry. Although there was a considerable amount of activity in the last quarter of the century, as new titles poured on to the market and the advertisers steadily increased, it was an unscientific period with very little factual information. All the magazines naturally made extravagant claims about their circulations and their readership but it was not until 1931 that the Audit Bureau of Circulations arrived.

It must have been a bewildering time for the advertiser. As Cynthia White records, 48 new titles were launched in the 20 years between 1880 and 1900. Some were extremely ephemeral but others survived for varying lengths of time. Indeed, *The Lady* (1885) is still with us today – the oldest surviving women's magazine. This latter period of the nineteenth century was rich indeed in the variety and quality of new titles. The ones which survived for more than token appearances were such titles as *Home Chat*, launched in 1895 and surviving right through to 1958, *Home Companion* with a similar life span from 1897 to 1956, *Home Notes* 1894–1957, *The Ladies' Field* 1898–1928, *The Ladies' Review* 1892–1908, *The Lady's Realm* 1896–1915, *Weldon's Ladies' Journal* 1879–1954, *Woman's Life* 1895–1934, *The Young Gentlewoman* 1892–1921, *Madame* 1895–1913. Other titles published were *Princess* (1890), *Schoolmistress* (1881), *Woman* (1890), *Young Ladies' Job* and the *Lady Cyclist* (1895). You can take almost any permutation of the words Lady, Woman, Girl, Home, World, Realm, Life, Friend, Letter, Own, Journal, Wife, Fashion, Companion, Mother, Young and Pictorial, mix them up to produce any given combination, and you will find that a magazine was launched in the last two decades of the nineteenth century with that name. It says a lot for the inventive processes of successive generations of publishers that throughout the subsequent 70 years of women's magazine publishing the invention of new title names has continued with surprisingly little repetition.

The book publishers Cassell started a magazine in 1886 called *The Lady's World*: A Magazine of Fashion and Society. The following year a new editor was appointed – Oscar Wilde – who would only take on the task if the title was changed to *Woman's World*. He argued that the former title was tainted with vulgarity and was misleading, being inapplicable to 'a magazine that aims at being the organ of women of intellect, culture and position.' Wilde's editorship was to last only two years. (This *Woman's World* is not to be confused with the same title which was launched in 1866, a severely practical magazine which eschewed fashion and gave prominence to politics, the fight for women's suffrage and disestablishment. It changed its title in 1869 to *The Kettledrum*, subtitled The Woman's Signal for Action. This hardline feminist attack was not successful and it closed in 1870.)

The Lady started life badly until the editorship was taken up by Rita Shell in 1894. She introduced 'small ads', or classified, and they have remained a potent part of the magazine to this day. Without casting aspersion on its editorial abilities, one suspects that its longevity and present-day existence are due to its packed pages of announcements for seaside cottages, home helps and nannies rather than any lapel-grabbing editorial bite. But the title deserves a respectful salute because as well as holding the long-distance record as Britain's oldest women's magazine, it also enjoys the distinction of still being in private hands.

Early in the twentieth century came yet another *Woman's World*. This new *Woman's World* survived until 1958 and rather broadened the scope of many of its contemporaries, setting its cap at the office girl, the shop girl and the housewife. Perhaps it was the spearhead of the host of titles that were to flourish in the 1920s and 1930s aiming at just this market.

But as the market widened to take in the lower and middle classes, the latter end of the nineteenth century also saw the continual advance of the society magazine. Several titles were launched in this period including *The Gentlewoman*. One would like to feel that Mrs Pooter herself subscribed to at least one such magazine, and the rapid development of the inner suburbs and the parvenu, prosperous clerical and shop-keeper class, with all their pretensions and new servants, must have helped to fan the flames of this particular part of the market.

The younger end of the market was not neglected during this publishing boom. *Girl's Own Paper* was first published in 1880 and must be recorded as the original teenage magazine. In 1892 *The Young Woman* was published, this title aiming at a more egalitarian approach. *Woman's Weekly*, still with us today, was launched on 1 November 1911 priced at 1d. The year before had seen the launch of *My Weekly*, also extant, from D C Thomson of Dundee.

However, this era of magazine history is probably most marked by the influx of new titles which concerned themselves with the home and domestic life. Indeed, the titles of this period could not be more redolent of the hearth and kitchen: *Home Notes, Home Chat, Home Companion, Woman at Home, Ladies' Home Journal, Housewife*, are typical. They were what we would call today 'service magazines', aimed at the middle- and lower-market housewives who were primarily concerned with running their homes and their families. By and large they were successful publishing enterprises and two of them, *Home Notes* and *Home Chat*, lasted 60 years, finally succumbing in the late 1950s to old age and publishing economics. *Home Chat* was published by the brash young newcomer to the publishing scene, Alfred Harmsworth, later to become Lord Northcliffe. *Home Notes* was published by C Arthur Pearson. These two companies have a direct line of descent to the mighty IPC today, as Pearsons became Newnes and Harmsworth's company became Amalgamated Press (later Fleetway).

The publication of these two magazines, launched by the two most catalystic young men in Fleet Street, was one of the great milestones in the continuing progress of the industry. Both magazines had a major, popular success among middle-class readers and as the suburbs spread and the middle classes grew they could not go wrong.

The year 1910 saw another milestone established with the launch of *My Weekly* as a low-priced intimate magazine for the working woman. Still extant today, it is the second oldest surviving women's magazine in Britain (*The Lady* being the oldest; *The Tatler* never having been overtly a women's title), and is published by D C Thomson. As has frequently happened *My Weekly* was followed a year later by a very similar rival, *Woman's Weekly*. This again was a modest, low-priced formula of fiction, knitting patterns, cooking, problem page, etc, aimed at the same humble market. They are an interesting pair of magazines which by their sheer ingenious and simple formulae have survived two world wars, umpteen sweeping publishing revolutions and massive changes of public tastes. Not only are they the veterans of the game but *Woman's Weekly* actually now enjoys the biggest circulation of any women's magazine, outselling both its flashier IPC gravure rivals.

So as society changed, and Victorian England became Edwardian England, the publishing race continued. Society in its halcyon days before the First World War was amply provided with its own magazines which extensively covered its interests in the arts, the Court and the Season. *The Queen* magazine was still riding high, as were the high-class fashion magazines. By the outbreak of the First World War there were probably about 50 women's magazines on the market, and although the war took its toll of some of them, it was a fairly healthy collection of titles that had evolved to this stage of the history of women's magazines. Not only had women proved beyond all doubt to be avid and constant readers of magazines, both for information and entertainment, but the market had already discovered its own secret that has stood it in such prosperous stead down through the decades – to compartmentalise and specialise. Such a large market as women's magazines has always been sustained by its natural divisions: society, domestic, teenage, romantic, fashion, beauty, etc. There has always been at least one magazine on the market at any given time which a woman could relate to and identify with. The broad subjects, such as fashion, cookery, society, have sub-divided by readership – demographically, geographically, socially or by age.

A development just before the First World War to note was the acquisition of the National Magazine Company by William Randolph Hearst in 1911. The company was purchased from Evelyn Nash and its sole publication was *Nash's Magazine* with a cover price of 6d. This was a fiction magazine similar to the *Strand Magazine*. Hearst's first publication was a Sunday newspaper, *The London Budget*, on the lines of an American newspaper with separate magazine and comic sections. The venture was unsuccessful and ceased publication in 1913.

Nash's Magazine was to continue through the war as an outstanding success and also did a lucrative business with the sideline publication of its Harrison Fisher covers as separate prints. The National Magazine Company also purchased, just before the war, two old-established magazines, *Pall Mall* and *Vanity Fair*, but owing to paper shortages they were not published during the war. The latter title was to be resurrected 35 years later as a young fashion magazine.

So as Britain went to war the industry was in a strong position. The magazine story was only just beginning and sweeping changes were to echo down the years. Only three of the titles that survived at the outbreak of the First World War still survive today, but by 1914 a considerable industry had been established.

2

BETWEEN THE WARS

The decade after the First World War, which had taken its toll of several women's titles, seems not to have been particularly vibrant with magazine activity. About 25 new titles emerged during the 1920s, which was a fairly modest development considering the static period of four years of war and the major social and economic changes which had taken place since 1914.

The war obviously saw little magazine development except for one major event: the launch of the British edition of *Vogue* in 1916. *Vogue*, of course, is the definitive glossy fashion magazine representing the height of sybaritic opulence. It is perhaps a little ironic that it arrived on the British scene at the height of the greatest European war in history and probably at the point of the war when things looked at their gloomiest. *Girl's Mirror* was launched in 1915 and survived until 1933 and other titles of the actual war period were *Vanity* (1915) and *Betty's Weekly* (1916).

The 1920s saw the launch of some major titles as well as quite a crop of ephemeral rubbish. At the end of the war the circulation of *Nash's Magazine* began to decline in common with that of all fiction magazines but the National Magazine Company took a major step forward with the launch of the British edition of *Good Housekeeping*. The first number of this classic magazine was published in March 1922 at a cover price of one shilling. It was an immediate success and soon achieved a circulation of 150,000, carrying in some issues as many as 100 pages of advertisements. This was to be the first real taste in this country of the 'service' magazine, and it has often been claimed that the successful introduction of *Good Housekeeping* really created the women's magazine market in this country in the form that we know it today. The next National Magazine venture was *Pall Mall* in 1927 but this only lasted two years. *Nash's Magazine*, incidentally, eventually died in 1937. The National Magazine Company followed up the successful introduction of *Good Housekeeping* with the launch in 1929 of the British edition of *Harper's Bazaar*, which was a direct competitor to *Vogue*. These two glossy fashion magazines have been for decades bitter eyeball-to-eyeball rivals in the USA, but the battle was always rather one-sided in this country with the scales tipped heavily towards the more successful *Vogue*. (This situation became more balanced in 1970 when *Harper's Bazaar*, after a very lean period indeed in the 1960s, was merged with *Queen* magazine to become the contemporary *Harpers & Queen*.)

In 1919 *Homes & Gardens* was launched, the first of the new breed of middle-class journals wholly devoted to the domestic life. The market was a natural because the gardener, the cook and the maid had begun to disappear from the payrolls of the suburban home after the war. Here was a new market of still affluent householders who needed to take a direct interest in the maintenance and upkeep of their houses and their land. It was followed in 1920 by *Ideal Home*, published by Odhams Press.

The year 1919 also saw the introduction of *Peg's Paper*. This was the shopgirl formula which was to be so popular, with myriad titles right up to the Second World War. Magazines like *Peg's Paper*, which was an early casualty of the war in 1940, and its many imitators and successors over the decades, had a sort of matey, elder sister approach with lots of popular fiction of the crinkly-eyed-pipesmoker-meets-shopgirl-on-holiday type so that a million mill girls and shopgirls could dream along with their weekly ration of newsprint. They offered a sort of cushion against life when you could slip off your shoes, get out your toffees and float away on cloud nine. Another new title of the vintage was *Red Letter*, first published in 1929 and still among the living today.

Eve also came out in 1919 and survived to 1929 when it became *Britannia and Eve*, a successful glossy which ran until 1957. The original set its cap at the 1920s flappers and enjoyed a lively reputation during its decade of life.

Some quick flashes in the pan appeared in the 1920s: *Ladies' Home World, The Lady's Paper, Ladies' Times, My Lady Fayre, Home Mirror, My*

Favourite, Woman of the Day, Woman's Kingdom and *Femina* all came and went at lightning speed.

Two of the other 1920s' launches are still extant and flourishing today. *Woman and Home* emerged in 1926 and *Woman's Journal* in 1927. They have had their vicissitudes, but *Woman and Home* was selling more copies than any other women's monthly until the *Prima* explosion in 1986. It actually contains the bones of two other famous 1920s' productions – *Everywoman* (1924) and *Modern Woman* (1925). Both these titles survived until the 1960s when post-war costs caught up with so many titles as we shall see later in this book. Both titles were eventually merged into *Woman and Home*.

This period also saw two other titles which enjoyed reasonably long life spans, both permutations of the seemingly endless images of the home and the wife. There was *Wife & Home* in 1929 and *My Home* in 1928. The latter became *My Home & Family* but both titles have now disappeared into *Woman and Home*, which would seem capable of enfolding countless titles into its ample maternal bosom.

The 1920s also saw the early rumblings of a sub-industry of women's magazines. This was largely an American inheritance of the confession/scandal/true story genre which has always been a successful down-market formula and has manifested itself in many forms. *True Story* arrived in 1922 as an American import.

True Story, and its close companion *True Romances*, have an interesting background. The story began in the 1920s when an 18-year-old Yorkshire girl, Mary Williamson, entered Great Britain's Perfect Woman competition organised by the American health and physical culture fanatic Bernarr Macfadden. She won and shortly afterwards became Mrs Macfadden. Macfadden was already publishing a magazine in the USA called *Physical Culture*, which attracted a great deal of readers' correspondence. As so many of the letters involved the readers' problems and failures and successes of their personal lives, Mary Macfadden had the foresight to see that these highly personal revelations could form the basis of a different and new sort of magazine with all the stories written in the first person. They launched *True Story* on these lines and its immense success was quickly followed by its 'me-too', called *True Romances*. (The 'me-too syndrome is quite simple. A publisher looks at the market, sees a publication which is doing very nicely, decides that he can do the same thing and that the market can stand a competitor.)

Both magazines were dominated by the ethos of true love and happy marriage. Unfortunately, the married life of the founders was less idyllic and Mary returned to England leaving Mr Macfadden the freedom to pursue his rather eccentric life-style. (He later parachuted into the Seine at the age of 80, amongst many other exploits.)

In 1943 the Argus Press acquired the British rights of both the magazines, adding a third title to the stable in 1956 – *Woman's Story*. All three titles carry the whole range of the usual women's features but the *raison d'être* of the magazines has always been the problem pages and the personal story. The stories in *True Story* and *True Romances* are all based on real life experiences with the actual names of the people changed. They are a mixture of British and American authors, but all stories are anonymous.

So the 1920s produced a mixed bag of new titles rather than new directions, but it was a period not without significance for the women's magazine industry. The war had broken down many of the old class barriers and a new egalitarianism was emerging. The lives of women were broadened and new markets were being created. The advertising industry began to get organised with the birth of all the new and subsequently famous advertising agencies, with their bright new techniques and ever-growing army of clients who wanted to become household names.

The publishing companies began to form themselves into considerable-sized firms like Odhams Press, Newnes, Amalgamated Press, D C Thomson and the National Magazine Company. The real battles for readers and advertising were really just beginning.

Woman's Friend saw the light of day in 1924, published weekly for 2d by C Arthur Pearson (later Newnes). It was the customary formula of fiction, knitting, a few little poems, patterns, cooking, health and babycraft problems, a horoscope and a problems page. Enormously successful, it ran until 1950 when it was merged with *Glamour*.

It is interesting to analyse a contemporary copy of a magazine like *Woman's Friend* to see what you got for your 2d. The issue examined is 1 January 1938, consisting of 36 pages. Thirty-two pages were editorial, two and one-third were 'house advertisements' (free advertisements for other magazines in the group such as *Woman's Sphere*, Enid Blyton's *Sunny Stories* and *Screen Pictorial*) and one and two-thirds were paid-for advertisements. The advertisements quota was solidly dominated by a back page for Atora Beef Suet and small advertisements for the ubiquitous H Becker's piano lessons, Phillips Dental Magnesia and a discreet offer of a free sample of Triumph Female Pills – 'Safe, Sure, Speedy for Irregularities'. Other 1930s' issues of *Woman's Friend* show the same sort of page breakdown. This particular issue kicks off straight away with a royal baby picture on the cover, embellished with an Ursula Bloom poem. The baby was Princess Alexandra of Kent. There is a story ('The woman who stays at home . . . does she wonder about the women who don't? About the women her husband meets during office hours? A story that will appeal to every wife'), a Nova Pilbeam interview, a jumper knitting pattern, a serial by Lady Troubridge, some party dishes ('Macaroni and Turkey Réchauffé'), Your Fate for 1938 from the cards, Jane's Journal, A Day in the Life of an Ordinary Housewife, Ask Susan March (red face, wart inside nose and constipation are three of the problems), Dr Mary Advises You, which contains a heartfelt problem from Mrs A. of Rotherham:

> My daughter is rather a reserved girl and has a nice young man. They want to get married but she is very innocent and asks me how babies come and things she should know. Being shy myself I can't explain, and reading your talks I hope you can help me to get some kind of an illustrated book which will help her to know these things.

There are two more stories, a clairvoyant's guide to the week ('A girl who is handed a caption from a Christmas cracker containing a love rhyme may rest assured that her love affairs will go very happily and smoothly'), The Housewives Club (*Q.* 'How can I be certain of keeping my party frock clean when washing up on Christmas Day? *A.* By wearing an old mackintosh . . .), Percy Puffins Play Page and Fireside Friends by The Shadow Woman ('Don't you find it easier to discuss your problems in the flickering light of the fire? That's why the Shadow Woman is the right person to help you.')

This was the mix of the 'twopenny mag' beloved by shopgirls and housewives. A similar recipe was *Woman's Pictorial*, issued from 1919 onwards by Amalgamated Press. This went to the expense of a colour cover but inside was strong on fiction, patterns, housewife's hints and recipes; big on babies and the inevitable problem page. The issues we have seen appeared healthy with advertising, a proportion of about 30 per cent.

Of course, another ingredient across the board of the cheaper magazines was the royal family, or 'Knit your own Royal Family' in the immortal phrase evoked by Jocelyn Stevens when he owned *Queen* magazine in the 1950s. It was fortunate that royalty obliged by being so fecund in the 1920s and 1930s. There were the two royal princesses Elizabeth and Margaret Rose, whose activities were so keenly followed. The Gloucesters and the Kents also produced children who were instant 'copy' for the magazines and not a move or a nuance was lost on the twopennies. The minutiae of their lives were recorded in constant reports, from their clothes to their hobbies, their holidays and their schooldays. These were not the days of the scandals or the innuendos. The army of readers was regaled with the prosaic trivia of somebody else's family life. Here's a lapel-grabbing example from *Woman's Friend*'s 'Let Us Gossip' page:

Tweeds for the Princesses
 A reminder that the Princesses Elizabeth and Margaret Rose are growing up into big girls will, I've just been told, be given by new winter coats that are being made for them to wear after Christmas.
 These coats are more substantial than the little Princesses have worn up to now. They're being made of real honest-to-goodness Harris tweed, from some length of the fragrant homespun which the Queen bought for herself at a recent exhibition. One pattern that particularly pleased Her Majesty was a black and white dog-tooth check – rather like the familiar Scots 'Shepherds Plaid'. It's likely I hear that some of this length will be made up for the Princesses.

It took 'Crawfie' in the 1950s to set a new standard of inside revelations about the royal family but the 'Palace Industry' has provided meat and drink for the monthly and weekly women's magazine since the mid-1920s. They are today as essential to the mix of the weeklies as the problem page or sex.

Photogravure

The 1930s was a most significant decade in the development of women's magazines. First and foremost, it saw the arrival of the three great weeklies, *Woman's Own* from Newnes in 1932, *Woman's Illustrated* from Amalgamated Press in 1936 and *Woman* from Odhams in 1937. *Woman* is particularly noteworthy because it was the first women's magazine to be fully produced by photogravure. Not only had a new standard of printing arrived that would almost overnight make the pulp weeklies look very drab and almost dilettante, but the whole concept of the process of gravure printing was geared to huge numbers of copies. Photogravure is an expensive process in preparation but the rewards come in the running-off of copies by the million with 'run-on' costs getting appreciably less as the run mounts. Here was a whole new ball game – for the first time magazines could move into almost the same league as newspapers and could aim for a truly mass market. A successful mass market also meant, of course, mass advertising and women's magazines could now move away from the rather squalid reproduction of the small-run magazines of the 1920s with their repetitive advertisements for sanitary products, custard powders, patent medicines and the like and move into the big, glorious world of superb colour printing and the large budget advertisers. So the advent of *Woman*, to be followed so shortly afterwards by the outbreak of the Second World War, shattered the old magazine industry and began the revolution.

Early copies of *Woman's Own* show it to be the same formula as its predecessors. A representative issue, dated 21 July 1934, published at the familiar cover price of 2d, bears a monotonous resemblance to any of the other popular magazines published ten years before. There were 36 pages, of which nine were paid-for advertising. But the distinguishing mark from its competitors is the inclusion of an eight-page section 'incorporated by means of Bell Punch Company's Intersettor.' The magazines was printed by the Sun Engraving Company of Watford, and although the gravure pages look no more attractive than sepia ink on rather better paper, they stood out like a sore thumb among the uncoated paper and letter-press printing of the rest of the magazine.

The introduction of *Woman* on to the market must have been shattering for the rest of the women's magazines. By the outbreak of war in 1939 it was selling 750,000. The editor was the famous and inventive Mary Grieve, who was to reign on the *Woman* throne right through to the 1960s.

Woman's Illustrated was in the same mould as *Woman's Own* which had preceded it by four years. It was never the success of its two illustrious sisters and was only selling about 150,000 by the outbreak of the war. Its circulation showed a consistent and steady climb through the post-war years, peaking in 1958 at almost 900,000. But this was the period when its two big rivals were selling two and a half million and three and a half million and it couldn't compete with that pace. It died in 1961 when its circulation had declined to 676,000.

Odhams also brought out *Mother* in 1936, which was launched with the highest hopes. Its very title and contents obviously set its own limitations but it achieved a creditable sale of 115,000 at the beginning of the war although, apart from the 1960s when its circulation hovered around its 1939 figure, it has more often than not sold under 100,000.

Other 1930s' activities included some 'quickies' like *Ladies' Only* (1933–5), *Miss Modern* (1930–40), *Woman's Fair* (1935–41) and *Woman's Mirror*, which appeared in 1934 only to be merged into *Woman's World* in 1935. These latter two titles have been heard of since in other reincarnations. *Woman & Beauty* was launched in 1930 and survived through to 1963. Its circulation declined steadily to its deathbed figure of a derisory 73,000.

Just before the war came one more women's magazine that would buy itself some piece of this involved history. This was *Housewife* and it came from the new publishing house of Hulton Press. Hulton's had seen instant success in 1938 with the weekly illustrated magazine *Picture Post*, the sleek and clever competitor to Odhams' *Weekly Illustrated*. (Hulton's also started *Lilliput* and bought *Farmer's Weekly*.) *Housewife* began life pocket-size, like its famous stable mate *Lilliput*, but later moved up to a more conventional format. It survived until 1967, dying as part of the IPC empire. Like many of the major magazines mentioned in this chapter we will be studying its decline and fall later in the book.

So came 1939 and the war. Perhaps there is a parallel between the crudity and confusion of the early period of the 'phoney war', and its eventual super-efficiency and professionalism, with the magazine market up to the war and after it. The women's magazine battlefield had been a positive clutter of titles, with an amazing number of sudden deaths littering the field. The general editorial standard of the pulp weeklies was rather appalling and naïve. But perhaps with all their ingenuousness they made a lot of women happy, or certainly put an element of cheerfulness and instruction into some very drab lives. Then came the war and afterwards the 'super powers' took over. As we will see, the slaughter moved from gunfire to atomic holocaust and, although the products have improved out of all recognition, maybe the contemporary industry is a no happier place than in the less demanding 1920s and 1930s with their letterpress printing, squared-up half-tones and the ability to survive with small circulations and low budgets.

THE FIFTIES

The women's magazine industry, like so many other businesses and activities, was frozen by the Second World War. The government allocated a paper rationing system which operated on a pre war average usage. Therefore the magazines that survived the advent of the war (and many gave up the ghost during the early months) had no freedom at all to expand, either in issue size or circulation development.

Of course, like newspapers, general magazines and books, women's magazines enjoyed an incredible boom during the war years. Reading matter was hard to get, and then of such a limited size that everything printed enjoyed a ready market. Women on the home front, and in the services, mopped up the magazines which hit the bookstalls. Advertising too was severely curtailed in all media and the magazines had to accept their share of the ubiquitous government information advertising. Media planning by the advertising agencies went out of the window – advertising space became one of the war's scarce commodities and advertisers bought whatever they could find. This gave an artificial boost to the lives of some magazines which might otherwise have died.

The immediate post-war period saw the continuation of the restrictions and shortages. Paper rationing continued with the same allocations which had been frozen in 1939. The export drive occupied British industry, so the severe shortage of capital goods with the continued rationing of clothes and food meant that the advertising business had little to advertise on the domestic scene. As in the war, there were many token advertising campaigns which actually encouraged the consumer to cut down on the use of the product, if they could get it. Alternatively, they simply had to be content with futuristic promises. The magazines and newspapers curtailed their advertising pages to the minimum and the actual areas of space available to advertisers were as spartan and as 'utility' as the goods in the shops.

So the immediate post-war years were hardly a period of expansion for the women's magazines. In 1946–7 there were about 25–30 leading weekly and monthly magazines on the market. This was a vacuum period – several titles had not survived the outbreak of the war and the big post-war expansion had not yet begun. Yet, if they had been given the paper and the capital, these should have been exciting days for the women's press. Millions of women had seen wartime service in the forces or the factories. Life had changed dramatically and considerably for the average younger woman and all sorts of new opportunities for jobs and life-styles were now possible. There was a new Labour government creating a mood in the country to make life better for a great many people than it had been before the war. This was a new dawn, a new awakening, a new chance for a new sort of life. Here was a golden opportunity to enthuse and lead these women into a new Valhallah and prevent them from slipping back into the old way of life. With the wisdom of hindsight it is difficult to understand, looking through some of the magazines of the period, why this nettle was not grasped.

However, two particular magazines certainly used this post-war period to bring about their own metamorphosis. *Woman* had a circulation just touching the magic million in 1946 and its arch-rival *Woman's Own* stood at nearly 700,000. They were lucky because they had two great advantages in their bid to capture the new mass audience that was beginning to build up. They enjoyed a good quality photogravure printing and they had dedicated and expert editors. Mary Grieve was still firmly at the helm of *Woman* and the extrovert and articulate James Drawbell was at Newnes to take *Woman's Own* into exciting new stratospheres. For both of them the opportunities were limitless. The competition was looking pretty faded and the 'big two' had the chance to capture the audience of young women with a new, entertaining formula.

Without wishing to pre-empt our story chronologically, the actual achievements of these two magazines have to be admired when one considers that by the mid-1960s *Woman* achieved a miraculous circulation of 3,200,000 and *Woman's Own* a high of 2,272,000. Moreover

22

these circulations were achieved during a period of intense competition in the market. Less mercurial, but eventually more steady,
was the quiet upward success of *Woman's Weekly*. This was the drab little
sister compared with its flashy, glossy siblings, but with its modest
aims it crept up from an immediate post-war circulation of 750,000 to
a 1987 figure of 1,300,000. And it had come all the way from 1911. For
decades its simple two-colour formula had been unchanged but in
February 1967 it switched to full colour. This enhanced the magazine
enormously and at the same time broadened the editorial outlook to
appeal to a wider age group. However, the basic recipe of a story,
problem page, knitting pattern and a general all-over 'cosy' feel was
wisely retained.

D C Thomson's *My Weekly* also survived the war and by 1946 had a
circulation of just under 200,000. It has always disdained such lux-
uries as quality paper and printing and has looked emphatically and
rather proudly down-at-heel. Certainly there has been no major
escalation and in the mid-1950s its circulation reached some incredible lows. But it has always been a survivor and a fighter and today its
circulation of over 600,000 still makes it a cheap buy for the
advertisers.

So the big two gravure weeklies, under their two impressive editors,
were poised for their major breakthrough into big-time publishing. In
rereading contemporary copies it is noteworthy that, in general terms,
not a lot of new ground was broken. They were really quite content to
tread the familiar and proven ground of the subjects which were
well-known to women readers. But techniques were certainly new: the
glossy gravure pages showed more and more colour – in both the
editorial and advertising pages – and the use of brilliant artwork. They
looked good. Another new element also appeared – entertainment.
These magazines began to be fun and presented each week a more
total mix of instructive and entertaining features. After the drab
monotone years here was twopence-worth of cheerfulness, well presented and attractive to read. Rather more outspoken problem pages
were introduced, beginning to mention subjects and situations which
even The Shadow Woman had not put into print. Perhaps when the
reader picked up her *Woman's Own* the first page she turned to was
Mary Grant, with all those readable questions and answers. Then, of
course, there was dear old Beverly Nichols and good old Godfrey
Winn, slugging it out pussy-cat by pussy-cat. When you reread their
gentle homilies today you realise just how readable they were, just

how right for the moods of the time and for their intended readership. Although it is easy to scoff at them now, the fact is that nobody has taken their place. No one is writing that sort of column week by week as well as they did.

The other section of the market which survived the war was the story titles – weeklies like *Miracle*, *Lucky Star*, *Oracle*, *Red Star* and the monthlies like *True*, *True Story* and *True Romances*.

Also emerging from the war were a few of the 'glossies'. *Queen* and *Vogue* were still there, as was *Harper's Bazaar* and *The Tatler*. And the 'home press' was still intact. *Good Housekeeping* had a circulation of 120,000, and *Housewife* was riding high with over 270,000 – a circulation which in fact was to be the highest in its history. From the end of the war onwards its fortunes steadily declined. *Ideal Home* and *Homes & Gardens*, however, were still going strong.

In the immediate post-war period there were two important developments which were to have the most profound effect on the evolution of the women's magazines. The first took place in 1947 when Princess Elizabeth married Prince Philip of Greece. Their romance and marriage were straight out of the fairy-tale books and created a mood of gaiety and celebration amidst the greyness and dullness of austerity-ridden Britain. The arrival of children provided ideal editorial fodder for the popular magazines of the 1950s and 1960s. The 'Royals' industry was now to march forward with renewed vigour, and the editors of Odhams, Newnes and Amalgamated Press were to be supplied with never-ending streams of royal copy and royal photographs to boost their circulations. It is interesting to ponder the state of some of the popular magazines in the post-war years had King Edward VIII not abdicated in 1936 but lived childless to a ripe old age.

The other development was even more significant. As the hordes of servicemen returned to civilian life they married the girls they had left behind, or returned to the wives they had married during the war. A great avalanche of previously frustrated parenthood was now about to take place, resulting in the babies who became the 'post-war bulge' – the teenagers of the 1960s. This great army of adolescence was in time to create its own mini-industry of teenage magazines.

As recorded, the 1940s had not been a decade of magazine development but one important title was launched in 1949 – *Vanity Fair* from the National Magazine Company. This magazine must not be confused with the famous old Victorian title noted for its political caricatures, but was in effect a fashion magazine for the shorthand typist and as such was an immediate success. It appealed to a generation which had been starved of fashionable clothes and it is surprising, in retrospect, that it should have been so successfully launched during a period of clothes rationing. *Vanity Fair* had been preceded in 1946 by a magazine called *Mayfair* which was also aimed at the younger market; this only survived until 1950, but it should be recorded here as the first true attempt after the war to recognise presciently the coming teenage market – perhaps it suffered the fate so often experienced by the pioneer.

Vanity Fair, however, cleverly edited by Phyllis Bailey, offered the teenager and the younger market exactly what they wanted at prices they could afford. Up to that time the fashion magazines had had little relevance for the younger reader – the models, clothes and prices in *Queen*, *Harper's Bazaar* and *Vogue* were just too up-market and the styles too mature for them to want to wear even if they could afford them. *Vanity Fair* deserved to succeed and in its own way it pioneered a new type of magazine, becoming so successful that the National Magazine Company later increased its frequency to 16 issues a year to absorb all the fashion advertising that was in the market. Its circulation peaked in 1956 at 238,000, a considerable achievement in those days for such a specialised magazine; it rode high during the rest of the 1950s and the early 1960s but then began a slow decline in circulation and advertising volume. Surviving the birth of the new teenage magazines, it was ably edited in the late 1960s by Hazel Evans and subsequently Audrey Slaughter. But a financial point of no return was reached in the early 1970s when its circulation of 120,000 was insufficient to attract the quantity of advertising it needed to survive. *Vanity Fair* died in 1972, the month after National Magazine Company launched their sensationally successful *Cosmopolitan*.

Births

The next important launch (after *Vanity Fair* started in 1949) was also from the National Magazine Company: the highly individualistic *She*, with a new larger page size, which appeared in 1955. This was a particularly significant year for the magazine industry as it saw the birth of commercial television. *She* was created by Michael Griffiths, who was to remain its art director for over 20 years, and was a new concept in British magazines – big, bold and rather brassy. Here was a new idea –

a general features magazine for women with a strong, light, humorous flavour. The original editor was Joan Werner-Laurie, considerably helped by Nancy Spain. (They were both tragically killed in a private plane crash on their way to the Grand National a few years later.)

She was a strong formula magazine with its format and logo owing not a little to the then highly successful photo journalism magazine *Picture Post*. It was a unique mix of brash and down-to-earth articles and pictures with an inherent thread of British vulgarity. It was printed on cheap uncoated paper and achieved a remarkable circulation of over 300,000 copies by the 1970s. Editorially it was a mishmash of punning headlines, frank sex articles, peculiar photographs and rude jokes. It was like no other contemporary women's magazine of the 1950s and back in 1955 the pundits were not overhopeful of its survival. It had the effect of a fast-talking, loud-suited, red-nosed uncle in the rather gentile drawing room of the women's magazines of the day. As its career progressed, under the editorship of Michael Griffiths and his wife Pamela Carmichael, it pioneered sex in women's magazines. It ran extracts from Dr Reuben's book 'Everything you wanted to know about sex . . .' long before *Cosmopolitan* moved into the business. *She* created its own loyal readership and picked up some enviable readership figures, becoming a profitable advertising success. It was to show some decline in the 1980s, as we will see, but is now showing a remarkable come-back under the editorship of Joyce Hopkirk.

The year 1955 also saw the launch of *Marilyn*, which was to live for a decade. This was another foretaste of the teenage boom which was yet to come in earnest. There was a slight increase in such titles in the mid-1950s – *Mirabelle* in 1956, *Romeo* and *Valentine* in 1957, *Roxy* in 1958. City Magazines brought out *Boyfriend* in 1959. The first four of these were down-market fiction titles which have all bitten the dust. *Boyfriend* was an attempt at a more all-round teenage formula which became merged, via *Trend*, into *Petticoat* in 1967.

The year 1958 was the year of new weeklies. Because *Woman* and *Woman's Own* were doing so well (both at their historical circulation peaks) their publishers, Newnes and Odhams, hit upon a formula to syphon off some of the colour advertising that was proving almost an embarrassment to them in the quantity being offered. Commercial television was not yet fully in its stride but already the famous old general weeklies like *Picture Post*, *Everybody's*, *Illustrated* and *John Bull* were either staggering to the graveyard or had actually expired. This meant that the major mass women's weeklies were virtually the only media available for the big-budget colour advertiser. The queue, metaphorically curling down Holborn and the Strand, was formed by advertisers anxious to invest in the colourful gravure weeklies. The solution, hit upon by the publishing giants, was to produce an additional mini-*Woman* and mini-*Woman's Own*; Newnes produced *Woman's Day* and Odhams *Woman's Realm*. They were established in 1958 with circulation ambitions of one million each. Not only would they provide an overflow for the giant advertisers but would also open up a new medium for the smaller colour advertisers who could not afford the high-flying rates of the two big titles.

Woman's Day was the unluckier of the two. It began with the requisite print order of one million but showed a consistent drop until it was kindly put out of pain in 1961 with a circulation, quite unsatisfactory by the standards of those palmy days, of only 888,000. Looking at a copy today it is not hard to see why it never took off. It was a pallid imitation of *Woman's Own* without individual character or any visible reader identification. The issues we have seen are rather thin and with a marked weakness of advertisement support, particularly for those lush advertising days. Odhams fared very much better with *Woman's Realm*, which had the advantage of a good editor, Joyce Ward, and aimed more at the domestic market than *Woman's Day*. Its first year's circulation topped the 1.3 million mark so that it was immediately stronger as an advertisement medium than its rival. It peaked in circulation in 1962 at 1,424,000, but its story becomes gloomy after that high point and shows a steady downward path over the ensuing 15 years, with a circulation of 625,000 in 1987. Commercial television, of course, took its toll of so much of the advertising available in the 1950s. The five big women's weeklies have all shown a dramatic accumulative drop since the healthy days of the 1960s. In the decade 1965–75 the four IPC weeklies (*Woman*, *Woman's Own*, *Woman's Realm* and *Woman's Weekly*) showed a total drop of three million sales. Part of the explanation must be laid at the door of steady price increases which constantly niggled away at sales, but it appears likely that the editorial, by and large, has lacked a lot of the sparkle and style of the Drawbell-Grieve days. Moreover, the tendency of the market since the late 1950s has been for more specialised monthlies, the success of which has also helped to erode the previously strong position of the weeklies.

Another big event of the 1950s was the birth of *Woman's Mirror* to join the battle of the weeklies. Launched in 1956, it was to be one of

27

the flops of the industry. It began life as a Sunday newspaper – *Woman's Sunday Mirror* – which today seems rather a female chauvinistic project, but subsequently became a woman's weekly whose life span lasted exactly a decade – the circulation hovering just over or just under the million with its peak during the first year of 1,179,000. It was to be relaunched in 1965 to reflect the then contemporary vogue to shock and was summarily executed by IPC. We will discuss this relaunch in the next chapter.

Deaths

Having examined the births of the 1950s we now have the gloomier task of picking over the bones of the deaths. If, for convenience, we count the 1949 *Vanity Fair* as a 1950s' launch, then there were 11 births in the decade, but sadly only two of them, *She* and *Woman's Realm* are still with us today. There were 12 deaths, and it is interesting to peer into the coffins. Some received a kiss of life by being merged into sister publications, whereas others received the clean chop of the executioner's axe. We feel that the latter method of dispatch is kinder and more honest. The tinkering of merged titles is a publisher's sleight of hand to transfer the readers from the expired title to the living one and, with a bit of luck, some of the advertisement contracts may be retained. It is usually a confidence trick on the reader who seldom recognises anything of her old magazine in the new title she has been exhorted to buy.

Three of the saddest deaths of the 1950s were the old Victorian trio *Home Notes* (1894–1957), *Home Chat* (1895–1958) and *Home Companion* (1897–1956). They found themselves washed up on the 1950s beach like obsolete Victorian sailing ships quite unable to cope with modern life. Perhaps they had really out-lived their usefulness by the time the Second World War broke out in 1939, but because of the paper shortage and allocation system had managed to survive a couple of decades on borrowed time. They were really just too cosy and, folding up their mittens and making themselves a last cup of tea, gracefully faded away.

Another Victorian relic was *Weldon's Ladies Journal*, which had seen the light of day in 1879 and survived right through to 1954. It became merged into *Home* and that title in turn was incorporated into Newnes' *Homes & Gardens*.

Woman's Pictorial had a messy death in 1956. It had soldiered on since 1920 and had been a good money-maker for Amalgamated Press for many years. Again, its formula and image simply could not coexist with the modern pace of the newer magazines. It was merged ignominiously into AP's *Home Chat* in 1956, and its new mother was itself scrapped in 1958 as we have just seen.

Woman's Friend, launched back in 1924 by Pearsons (later Newnes), just managed to survive into the 1950s. It was another tired old war-horse that had faithfully served its master but could gallop along no more. In 1950 it was put into the failing *Glamour*, which in 1956 was itself swallowed by *Mirabelle*.

Other 1950s' deaths were *Modern Home* which had started life in 1928 and was merged into Newnes' *Modern Woman* in 1951, *Ladies' Mirror* (1903–54), *Woman's World* (1903–58) and *Miracle* (1935–58). A 'glossy' also died in 1957 – *Britannia & Eve* – which dated from 1929. This was part of the glossy magazine empire of Illustrated Newspapers whose collection was self-styled 'The Great Eight'. Others in the group included *The Tatler*, the *Bystander*, *Sphere* and *Illustrated London News*. The group was later sold to the acquisitive Canadian tycoon Roy Thomson who streaked through the 1950s buying any publication that he could. *Britannia & Eve* showed all the wrinkles of old age and was in the usual invidious position of not getting enough advertising to help prop up its ailing circulation.

So, the close of the 1950s presented a scene that was not over-hopeful for the industry. A lot of the old titles were running out of breath and lying down to die. The innovations and launches, with the very few exceptions we have discussed, failed to get a satisfactory grip on the slippery slopes of this fickle female market. Yet these were, after all, the boom days of Harold Macmillan's 'never had it so good' period. Paper became plentiful again as restrictions were lifted, and all rationing had come to an end. Even petrol came off 'pool' during the decade and the big brands returned to the market. The advertising agencies were attracting new talent and consumer goods were flowing back on to the home market. Print and paper were almost risibly in-expensive by today's standards. It is hard to understand, with all the wisdom of hindsight, just why the publishers – who were still independent companies and fiercely competitive – were so ploddingly slow to hack away at the old-fashioned, dated and ponderous titles and editorial styles in their attempts to stimulate the market with exciting new ideas.

Perhaps times were so good that they were happy with the *status quo*.

The press was not yet seriously concerned with the enormous impact about to be made by the electronic media. Life in Fleet Street tended to move at a comfortable amble, paying low salaries and failing to recruit the exciting talents who should have been attracted to all sides of the industry.

One of the other nagging problems of contemporary magazine publishing can also be laid at the door of the publishing bosses of the 1950s – the magazine cover price. Cover prices were for a long time kept artificially low because of the fear of losing circulation and hence, in turn, the lush revenues from advertising. There was a very real fear that women would react strongly to a penny or twopenny rise in their weekly or monthly magazine and in those dear old £sd days beyond recall it was a dictate of the trade that a magazine should only cost the price of a single coin. A threepenny piece, a sixpence, a shilling, a florin or at the top of the market a half-crown. This 'coinage factor' most certainly restricted overdue increases where today a small adjustment of a couple of pence would be made.

This is not to say that the public was insensitive to price rises. In the mid-1950s *Picture Post* was increased by Hulton's from its long accustomed 4d to 6d. Such was the public reaction against this iniquitous price rise that the publishers had to rapidly restore the price to 4d!

Basically, however, the argument is true and women have now grown accustomed to cheap magazines. No popular magazine in this country makes a profit out of its cover price – that is to say the physical cost of paper and print, coupled with the distribution costs, is not covered by the net price received by the publisher after trade discounts. The publisher's profit comes from the amount of advertising that he can sell in his magazine, and because of the low cover prices this means that the advertiser is paying too much towards the economics of the magazine in proportion to the reader. This leads to the vicious circle of the reader complaining that popular magazines carry too much advertising, but the publisher needing to fill his pages with enough advertising to pay his basic costs and provide his profit.

THE SWINGING SIXTIES

If women's magazines in the 1950s were disappointingly lacking in innovation and adventure, the 1960s compensated by being extremely volatile. In that decade 14 new magazines were launched and 11 folded. As we will see, the 11 defaulters were victims of the publishers' new euphemism – they were all 'merged' into more successful sister magazines.

This was also the era of the formation of the formidable International Publishing Corporation (IPC), a conglomerate of Odhams, Newnes, Hulton's and Amalgamated Press (as far as women's magazines and general titles were concerned), as well as countless other trade and technical publishing houses. As far as the big three consumer companies were concerned they were allowed to operate autonomously for a few years, more or less competitively, but by the end of the decade they were totally merged into one amorphous mass. We have serious misgivings that this was good for the publishing business, particularly as the later development of the Corporation led them into group advertising selling and the treatment of titles as brands in one great market. This effectively removed the competitive edge from certain sections of the business and competition is the life-blood of the magazine industry.

We will examine the deaths, or 'mergers', first and then look at the happier and more constructive picture of the decade. It is inescapable that any review of the women's magazine business in the 1950s and the 1960s is rather like one of those odd wartime newsreels of the battles of the western desert, showing the burned-out remains of tanks and armoured vehicles littering the sands as far as the eye could see.

Although this chapter started by revealing that 14 new magazines were launched in the decade, the sad truth is that exactly half of them are no longer with us, and one or two of them nose-dived very quickly.

1961 saw the departure of three titles. *Woman's Day* was the Newnes weekly which was launched in 1958 with such a touch of Eastern promise. Its circulation had declined sadly three years later and Newnes just had to let it slide away. With a proper sense of order they put it into *Woman's Own* – a case of the baby being returned to the womb. Two old-established titles 'went dark' that year. *Woman's Illustrated*, another weekly, had battled on since 1936 with a declining post-war circulation which ended up at only 676,000, totally unacceptable for a weekly and completely overshadowed by the big, glossy gravure competitors.

There is an inevitability in these deaths. The only way a publisher can remedy the red figures on his balance sheet is to increase his advertisement rates or his cover price, or both. But this merely increases the bleeding, because the fall-off in readers will probably accelerate on a failing magazine as the cover price rises and the advertiser is certainly not going to accept a rate increase for a falling circulation. Closure is the only solution to this vicious circle and so death came to *Woman's Illustrated*, which Odhams slipped quietly into *Woman*. Death came too to *Woman's Companion*, which had first appeared in 1927 but had always suffered from low circulation. At 177,000 it had to go, and being a weekly publication was merged into *Woman's Weekly*. So the three weakest were pensioned off into the three strongest weeklies.

The monthlies needed a spring-clean as well and IPC were equally ruthless about their fates. The first two on the list were *Home*, which was transported into *Homes & Gardens*, Newnes' solid domestic title, and *Woman & Beauty*, which went into *Honey*. *Woman & Beauty* had hit what must be the lowest circulation on record for a 'popular' title from a major publishing house: its deathbed figure was 73,000. Both these magazines disappeared in 1963.

Two years later came the sad departure of *Modern Woman*, with its lowest-ever figure of 134,000. Newnes had applied a lot of surgery to this title which always looked bright and professional, but the cause was patently hopeless and the publishers decided that the best place to put the magazine was into their similar formula *Everywoman*. This, too, was doing badly at 230,000 but Newnes apparently felt that *Modern*

Woman's readers might provide the necessary blood transfusion. It must have been the wrong blood group, however, as *Everywoman* itself departed this life in 1966, despite a slight upsurge in circulation to 278,000. *Everywoman*, including *Modern Woman*, was put into *Woman & Home*, which is rather like staring into an aquarium and seeing a little fish eaten by a bigger fish which is sublimely unaware of the shark coming up behind it – another example of the Russian doll technique when titles are absorbed into titles into titles, leaving the readers thoroughly confused.

Another such transfer was *Boyfriend*, which had been started in 1959 by City Magazines as the first of the teenage magazines. As we have seen this was moved into *Trend* in 1966, which itself was absorbed into the new *Petticoat* a year later, along with *Intro* – another teenage flop. *Petticoat* was eventually to be merged itself into *Hers*.

The year 1967 was the failure of yet another major title – *Housewife*. This was Hulton's pre-war title which had been transferred to Odhams Press when Hulton's was sold at the end of the 1950s. Here was a magazine with positive reader identification, a most explicit title, and an immediate post-war circulation of a quarter of a million which put it in the strongest position against its rivals. It was printed photogravure and like all the other publications from Hulton's Press (*Lilliput*, *Picture Post*, *Farmer's Weekly* and the famous Marcus Morris comics) was always editorially highly professional. Marcus Morris himself took a hand in its development while both he and the magazine still belonged to Hulton's, and it is sad to trace its career in the Odhams stable as one of hiccuping but declining circulation over the years. Its final circulation in 1967 was only 136,000 which, once again, was not enough to deliver the goods to the advertiser who was never at a loss for alternative choices of media. It may not be without significance that the highly successful parvenu from Thomsons, *Family Circle*, had started in 1964 and at the time of *Housewife*'s demise was selling one million copies a month through a new audience in the supermarkets. The average housewife had found a new and considerably less expensive champion. Odhams, continuing the merger game, interred *Housewife* into *Ideal Home*.

It was sad to see *Housewife* go as in the 1950s it had set a good pace, was competing fiercely against *Good Housekeeping* and at one stage had managed to overtake it in circulation. Perhaps if it had not become 'Odhamised' it could well have been able to stay the course in other hands.

The Business of Women's Magazines

In 1969 came the death of *House Beautiful*, published by the National Magazine Company. *House Beautiful* was another of the publications which the Hearst Corporation published successfully in the USA and produced an anglicised version in this country. Hearst and the National Magazine Company, like Condé Nast, have a most successful track record in developing American titles in the UK but *House Beautiful* was not to be one of their successes. In the USA it is a successful domestic title with a heavy emphasis on furniture and furnishings. The British version was aimed at the younger homemaker, which has always proved to be a difficult market, and it had to fight all the way against *Ideal Home*, *Homes & Gardens* and *Good Housekeeping*. It had difficulty in attracting sufficient readers or advertising and the National Magazine Company, in the only such event in their history, merged it into another title – the booming *Good Housekeeping*. *House Beautiful* had started in 1954 but never reached more than about 50,000 circulation.

Good Housekeeping is the personficiation of a successful magazine. It had established an enviable reputation before the war and was a considerable advertising and financial success. Its war record was sound, although it reduced in size to pocket format, becoming an important and useful morale booster for the home front. At the end of the war its circulation stood at around 100,000. In the 1950s and the 1960s it tended to retain its strong domestic image, although it was always ready to carry articles on contentious issues. It also had one absolutely unique selling proposition – the Good Housekeeping Institute – which had mirrored the American style and was founded two years after the magazine in 1924. The GHI Seal of Approval, abandoned in 1964 in the UK because of complicated consumerist legislation, was a phrase which passed into the language. The magazine began to change under the editorship of Laurie Purden in the 1960s, and subsequently Charlotte Lessing, who considerably widened its editorial scope to a life-style title while still cleverly retaining its food and cookery background. The editorial today is a wide admixture and beauty and fashion advertising balances the revenue from food. It is a big success and arguably the most profitable monthly women's title published in the UK. Laurie Purden moved on to IPC where she has enjoyed considerable success in resuscitating the ailing *Woman's Journal*.

We can now turn back to the 1960s to investigate the other side of the coin – the new magazines launched in that prosperous decade.

First we should examine some of the editorial and management thinking that was evolving at the beginning of the decade. IPC had won its battles by 1961 and the formation of this conglomerate now virtually dominated the market. On the outside were still important and profitable companies like the National Magazine Company, Argus Press, D C Thomson and the other Thomsons, but the women's market was obviously sensitive to any move made by the vast new organisation. It became obvious to all the pundits of the time that a whole new era in women's publishing had arrived. Masses of the old titles were dead or dying and the mergers, which bought time if nothing else, were not the answer to the challenges of the 1960s.

The 'new woman'

Big changes had taken place in the social lives of women since the war. By and large a great many of them were better educated, better paid, better dressed, better housed, more travelled and generally more sophisticated. Life was pretty good for a lot of people. Rationing was over, the world was at peace, television was a new strong life-force (making huge and permanent inroads into the cinema) and the women's magazine press had not yet truly taken up the exciting challenges of this new breed of woman. As well as closing and merging the old titles – and this process had to continue as the new rejected the old – publishers had to respond to the climate of what life was now really all about and launch new titles for this 'new woman'. The rewards would be reaped by the publishers who not only got it right, but got it right first. Who better than this great IPC conglomerate, full of tigers, to burst this great new bubble?

IPC fired the first shot in 1964 by commissioning the famous Dr Ernest Dichter of the Institute of Motivational Research in New York. Dichter had done a great deal of advertising and editorial work in the States. His specific task was to report on the future of *Woman's Own* but of course his studies were widely applicable to the whole development of the women's magazine reading market. His massive report had far-reaching consequences in IPC and across the business generally as he spelt out the necessity for the revitalisation of the women's press to suit the new woman. He reported that a whole new social and sexual revolution was arriving and that consequently the magazines must reflect these changes. We all quoted Dichter in those days and there is no doubt that his sweeping statements and conclusions contained ele-

RIDING HOUSE STREET LIBRARY, PCL
37-49 RIDING HOUSE STREET, W1P 7PT

ments of truth and wisdom. Even with hindsight one would find little
to contradict in his thinking except perhaps his forecast that class and
age would begin to matter less than a classification of readers by
interest. Although the latter is patently true today when every new
magazine has to be specialised in its appeal, it is equally true that the
biggest trend in the market over the last 40 years has been towards a
society where the greatest difference is between the generations. This
has been very evident in the magazine market in the past 15 years and
is paralleled in other spheres – clothes and music being outstanding
examples.

New methods need new people and a new appointment was made
by IPC – the post of editorial director was given to Clive Irving, a
whizzkid brought over from the *Sunday Times*. Backed by the Dichter
report, now almost the Holy Grail, Irving's task was to create new titles
to reflect the new thinking. A first attempt was to relaunch *Woman's
Mirror* which was not doing at all well after its transformation from
newspaper to magazine.

By the end of 1964 *Woman's Mirror*'s circulation dropped to below
the magic million mark, considered to be the basic circulation level
required by the big general women's weekly. Clearly it needed an
editorial blood transfusion and here was a classic case for the
Dichterian approach. In 1965 *Woman's Mirror* took off quite remarkably
in editorial terms. The opening salvo was a now famous issue which
had a cover photograph of a foetus and an inside story, so to speak, of
the development of an embryo in the womb. This was spectacular
stuff and caused quite a sensation.

The magazine was aimed hard and straight at a new generation of
women who were prepared to call a spade a spade and to look life
fairly and squarely in the eye. It had a heavy emphasis on pictures and
pulled no punches. There was also a change of name, at least on the
cover where it was designated by a prominent *WM*. (It is an interesting
sidelight that editorial directors who attempt to revolutionise an old
formula into something new and very modern like to abbreviate the
name in this way, almost trying to pass it over. *Everywoman*, before it
died, became redesigned as *E* and there was also an excellent men's
quarterly magazine brought out by John Taylor and the *Tailor & Cutter*
back in the 1950s called *Man About Town*. When taken over by
Haymarket Press it became *About Town* and then *Town*. Before it
became known as simply *3/6 Monthly* it disappeared, only to be quickly
relaunched by a new proprietor as *Man About* with a spectacularly

short life in this guise.)

However, a change of name, foetuses and all the new techniques of editorial and publicity departments could not save *Woman's Mirror*. Probably its ideas were too far advanced for its readership. From the moment of its regeneration the circulation continued to slide until reaching an all-time low of 858,000 in the first half of 1966. It was killed one evening, very suddenly and abruptly, and its corpse was moved into *Woman*, giving that magazine an immediate but albeit temporary burst of circulation.

Nova

In 1965 came the launch of a new magazine which was to personify everything that the new school stood for. *Nova* was launched in March 1965 by Newnes in a blaze of publicity. This was 'The New Magazine for the New Woman', and *Nova* set straight out to be the answer to the intellectual women's magazine needs. Here was a magazine for the woman who had received a good education but was now probably married with a couple of children, who found that the 'glossies' were superficial and the general run of domestic magazines were below her. After planting the bulbs and washing the kitchen floor she could settle down on her sofa and match her mind with the best who were contributing to *Nova*. *Nova* broke a lot of new ground. After the first two issues the editor was dismissed and Dennis Hackett, editor of *Queen*, was appointed to this exciting new post. With Hackett *Nova* acquired an immediate notoriety for its outspoken sexual articles and brilliant artwork. During the first couple of years *Nova* was arguably the best women's magazine to have been launched for a very long time. Frank, intimate, daring and never dull, it used words the like of which had not been sprinkled through the pages of a women's magazine before. And it was rewarded with not a little initial success. Although its peak circulation was only 160,000 achieved in 1966, which was the sort of figure which was killing its older rivals, it must be remembered that this was a 'class' publication aiming at a quality advertising market. It needed to collect the sort of advertising appearing in magazines like *Queen*, *Vogue*, *Harper's*, etc and this it did with disquieting success. The circulation figure placed it positively at the top of its particular heap; *Vogue* in 1966 was selling 130,000, *Queen* an estimated 50,000 and *Harper's* was staggering at the 40,000 mark.

The Business of Women's Magazines

The advertising agencies loved *Nova*, just as they loved the emergent newspaper colour magazines and had earlier been in love with *Queen*. *Nova* represented an art director's show place, a walking, breathing dossier of their artwork which would amuse and impress their artistic friends in NW2 and perhaps advance their careers. This was also the boom time of an advertising phenomenon, the massive colour campaigns for synthetic fibre advertising. Huge and prolific campaigns were being booked in the ABC1 women's magazines for a whole gamut of fibre advertisers like Bri-Nylon, Terylene, Dacron, Acrilan, Blue C Nylon and several other brands – to be answered in sizeable chunks by the natural fibres of the International Wool Secretariat and the Cotton Board. It was an advertisement director's bonanza and it breathed a great deal of welcome life into the traditional fashion glossies and the up-market general women's magazines. *Nova* was highly eligible for its share of this rich and extravagant advertising. Unfortunately, the synthetic fibre bubble burst at the end of the 1960s and after a last period of mopping up by the natural fibre campaigns the battlefield quickly became empty of contenders, creating a great aching void which was to have a profound effect on sections of the women's magazine market.

So *Nova* quickly established itself as a pace-setter for Newnes, and although its life was comparatively brief and the whole adventure ended in 1975 as an anti-climactic damp squib, there is no doubt that its advent and comparatively ephemeral career was to leave an indelible mark on the future development of the market. Newnes were so pleased with the initial success of their progeny that they promoted the editor Dennis Hackett to become the editorial director of all their women's magazines. He took with him his undoubted talent and applied a great deal of the *Nova* treatment to the other titles, including *Woman's Own*. This left *Nova* in a slightly vulnerable position as it was no longer unique in being the outrageous child saying such rude things in public. As *Woman's Own* started to use some of the same rude words and to take some of the gilt off the gingerbread, so the circulation of *Nova* began to take the old familiar pattern – downwards. Each six-monthly ABC figure showed a fairly steady decline. Gillian Cooke had succeeded as editor, but despite her valiant attempts to keep up the tradition of outrageous photography and shock tactics the magazine arrived at the point of no return. As her ideas grew wilder so the advertisers began to desert her pages and the magazine to commit the ultimate crime – dreariness. *Nova* became a rather depressing read, getting into gloomy if serious topics that only accelerated its downward spiral. One photograph in its latter months illustrates this point well; it showed a lady sitting on a lavatory in rather shabby surroundings and this photograph seemed to have been the last straw for some of the advertisers. It also attacked the royal family in one notorious issue, which must have alienated a chunk of its readers.

In an attempt to keep the magazine viable IPC reduced the page size, which had been one of its earlier attractions. There were two major reductions in format in the early 1970s, which brought it to little more than pocket size. Circulation reached an all-time low of 86,000 which spelt failure in very large letters. In the meantime, a very bright new star, *Cosmopolitan*, had appeared with shattering success and impact which delivered the final karate chop to the vitals for poor old *Nova*. It went out in 1975 with a whimper, a sad loss to the industry. Maybe its very title foretold its own eventual doom: the *Oxford English Dictionary* tells us that *Nova* is 'a star showing sudden large increase of brightness and then subsiding.'

Another magazine with great significance to our history in the early 1960s was *Queen*, which had been Samuel Beeton's brainchild in 1861. It had soldiered on through a century of publishing, always catering for the upper classes and their interests. In 1957 it was bought by Jocelyn Stevens, Edward Hulton's nephew, who was a millionaire by birth and up to the age of 25 had served in various posts in his uncle's old firm, Hulton Press. He acquired total ownership of *Queen* and after giving himself a year or two to settle in he made what he described as 'the great leap forward'. He brought in major talents like Mark Boxer, Bea Miller, Quentin Crewe and Francis Wyndham and transformed the old and dignified society magazine into a perfect reflection of what was to become 'the swinging sixties'. It was fortuitous that his brash and clever magazine coincided with the huge upsurge in entrepreneurial talents at the beginning of the 1960s. The time of tremendous movements and revolutions in the fashion scene, exemplified by the sudden and sensational rise of talents like Mary Quant, it provided unparalleled opportunities for the young entrepreneur to develop his talent for making money. *Queen* was in the forefront of all the bustle and excitement and became the parish magazine of the 'beautiful people' personified by the fast-developing Kings Road.

Queen's circulation never rose above 60,000 but, as with *Nova*, it became almost a cult with the art directors at the advertising agencies, carrying a volume of advertising far beyond its 'cost per thousand' capabilities. Able to sell fashion in the widest sense of the word, its brilliant (if often erratic) coverage of motoring, travel, food and drink, restaurants, jewellery, property *et al.* was matched and rewarded by hundreds of pages of advertising in these categories. As a fashion magazine, too, it became seriously accepted as a challenge to *Vogue* and *Harper's Bazaar*, though usually indulging in self-mockery with a distinct touch of iconoclasm.

Queen was also expert at producing a mix which has often been copied but never equalled. This was the blend of social irreverance and tart political comment alongside its more traditional role of recording the social scene via Jennifer's Diary. Its *avant-garde* fashion pages seemed to sit quite properly and happily alongside the pictures of 'chinless wonders' at the point-to-point or the dumpy adolescents at Queen Charlotte's Ball.

Jocelyn Stevens sold *Queen* in 1968, when he was lured away to join Beaverbrook Newspapers in an executive capacity. The magazine industry unhappily lost one of its most talented, if amusingly erratic, characters and it is sad to relate that up to the time of writing there has been no replacement of his calibre. The buyer of *Queen* was Michael Lewis, a millionaire printer and textile tycoon who after just over a year sold the magazine to the National Magazine Company, who combined it with *Harper's Bazaar* to make the successful *Harpers & Queen*. This is probably one of the few genuine mergers in the history of women's publishing, although it should in all honesty be recorded that the mixture still contains a considerable draught of *Queen*.

Harper's Bazaar had fared very badly since the war. It enjoyed a good reputation in the hat-and-white-gloves era in the early 1950s when its fashion voice was positive, but it had always lagged considerably behind *Vogue* in circulation, prestige and advertisement volume. During the 1960s it went through several changes of editor and editorial policy, and in 1967 was given to the editors of *She* for a year. However its circulation was now down to a dangerously low 37,000, and it was obvious to the National Magazine Company that extreme surgery was going to be required.

The resulting treatment was that good old standby, a relaunch. This was a major and expensive relaunch and some big guns were brought up to the barricades. Clive Irving led the attack, having now left IPC and gone into the business of 'magazine doctor'. He brought together a formidable team of editorial talent, including the irrepressible Molly Parkin as fashion editor and Joan Price as beauty editor. The result was 'The Return of the Beautiful Magazine' with the product immensely changed and geared right back to the 'Beautiful People'. Top business talent was also brought in and a considerable effort was made to bring the magazine seriously back into the market. A good measure of success was achieved during 1969 and 1970 when circulation improved and advertising sales dramatically increased.

At the end of 1970 the merger was made with Michael Lewis's *Queen*, and to date this combination of two good magazines has been most successful. The circulation has increased to 100,000 and advertisement volume is unbelievable by the old *Harper's Bazaar* standards.

While on the eddying swirls of the glossies in the 1960s we should also examine *The Tatler*. This suffered a strange twist of fate in 1966 when Thomsons – Roy, not D C – decided that this very famous old title was slipping dangerously. They had purchased the old Illustrated Newspaper Group with its string of glossies and *The Tatler* was the jewel in their crown. *Queen* had queered their pitch somewhat and, the biggest blow of all, Jocelyn Stevens had pinched the fairy off the Christmas tree by seducing Jennifer and her Diary away from them. Thomsons decided on draconian measures and plumped for complete surgery. *The Tatler* was closed and reopened as *London Life*, a trendy, pace-setting weekly full of the spirit of 'the swinging sixties'. The old *Tatler* was obliterated in favour of this parvenu which had only one fault – it was ahead of its time. Its editor was the young David Putnam of later film fame.

Again, it was the old vicious circle of no advertising because of no readers and the experiment died. *London Life* sank but, strangely enough, a lifeboat was on the horizon. The old *Tatler* title was rescued by Country Illustrated Magazine Group who saw the possibilities of restoring the old magazine to its former glory. They made a peppercorn payment to Thomsons and republished *Tatler*, complete with Regency fop and advertisements on the front cover.

The teenage market

Taking our story back to 1960, we can now examine the launch and positive success of another magazine that spawned in turn a whole new publishing pattern.

By 1960 the post-war-bulge babies had become teenagers. The

advertising business, and in particular Mark Abrams, was becoming aware of the vast market building up in this age group. Abrams defined a teenager as 'a person who is aged thirteen to nineteen unless he or she happens to get married before!'

At the beginning of the 1960s there was little in the visual media geared to cash in on this new market. Apart from *Vanity Fair*, which really had an older profile, there was only the 'comic cuts' area of teen reading like *Roxy*, *Valentine* and *Mirabelle* (billed in those days as The Romantic Three), but these were down-market demographically and editorially. There was a true 'gap in the market' and magazine publishers have never been backward in attempting to fill a void. Whether there is also a market in the gap is the publishers' conundrum.

The possibilities of this teenage market hit the advertising and publishing business like a bombshell. It was claimed that there were 7.5 million young people aged 12–24 and the market was growing. Almost overnight it seemed that there was a rich new vein to mine. We can do no better than to quote at some length from a teenage market feature written in the old *World's Press News* (now *Campaign*) of 4 March 1960 which positively gushed about the new world so recently discovered.

New Survey of £1,000 million market throws more light on teenage spending habits

The precious youngster of yesterday has become the precious teenager of today. The old cry of 'What are the youngsters coming to?' has given way to 'What are the teenagers coming to buy?'

It is true that today's teenager has never had it so good – nor so much money to spend on himself. In the past few years they have bought their way to the top and are paying a high price for their current importance – to the tune of nearly £1,000 millions a year. This is not the ceiling price, however. In the next two or three years two important factors will increase that figure by at least another £5 million. The first is the increasing number of school leavers, the second will be the end of National Service when thousands of 19–21-year-old youths will add their spending power to an already rich group of spenders.

More than £1,000 millions is a staggering figure but even more staggering is the fact that advertisers and their advisors have only recently realised the potential of the teenage market.

Last year London Press Exchange Ltd's research team, led by Dr Mark Abrams, made available a great deal of important teenage data. Now the results of another large-scale survey, said to be the biggest ever into teenage characteristics, are ready and they emphatically underline the power and the wealth of the new-rich teenage group.

Teenagers earn nearly £1,500 millions and after paying their board and lodging, often no more than a token payment to their parents, the average male has 7s 2d a day to spend: the female of the species something like 5s.

In London and the south-east the figure is slightly higher and, of course, in the working-class social grades it is greater than among 'top' teenagers. This is an important fact that advertisers must never forget – that there are two markets among teenagers.

Altogether there are some seven million teenagers whose spending amounts to something like £3 million a day. The average male spender buys approximately 11s worth of tobacco or cigarettes a week: the girl 3s 6d.

One only has to remember the modern trend in cigarette advertising to be aware of the fact that cigarette manufacturers are well up with the teenage habits.

The wardrobe is an important piece of furniture with both boys and girls. It is estimated that the female teenager, despite her apparent liking for nothing more than black jeans and sweaters, spends 6s 6d in every pound on clothes. The male, according to one research source, often spends more on clothing than his mother and sister put together.

The following is said to be not an unusual annual clothing expenditure for many young men teenagers:
6 suits at 10 guineas
12 shirts at £2 7s 6d
26 pairs of socks at 4s 6d
12 pairs of shoes at 3 guineas
4 'woolies' at £2
2 overcoats at £12 10s
A wardrobe fit for a king – or a princely teenager.

On beer the average male spends something like 6s a week: his teenager girl friend is more abstemious and drinking accounts for only 4d a week of her money. But on cinemas, theatres and discos, they spend together some £55 million a year.

No wonder it is 'Hooray for the teenager' where once it was something far less complimentary. We may not like their rock 'n' roll but manufacturers are getting to like their big roll of spending money.

Yet on the whole these same advertisers have failed abysmally to understand the teenagers, to find out what makes them tick and how to project themselves into the world of teenagers.

Mark Abrams, in his survey, said: 'Very few people over 35 can find it easy to meet successfully the challenge of serving the teenage market.' This was so very true and, to a lesser degree, is still true. Dr Abram's own findings made it easier and the application of the newest research data will make it easier to meet the challenge.

The publishers have not been slow to recognise this new and profitable market. There has been a spate of new weeklies for youngsters, e.g. *Boyfriend*, *Mary*, *Princess* etc. and soon there will be *Date* from the Odhams stable.

These new weeklies are aimed at different sections within the young age-group but the main editorial interests are likely to be music, films, clothes, travel, food and drink.

Incidentally, it appears that the only way to guarantee a successful launch is to give away a disc or picture of the most recent teenage idol with each copy!

The national dailies now publish a disc page as regularly and solemnly as they print book pages. News items and pictures of teenage fashions appear regularly, which certainly pleases the tailoring and shoe trades. They know that the big money market for clothes and shoes is now to be found among the nearly 8 million unmarried young people who know what they like, who won't accept second best and have the money to buy what they want.

This applies not only to fashions, but to the purchase of beer, wines, cigarettes, sweets, in fact to all commodities which constitute to younger people the idea of 'having a good time'.

Many manufacturers have shown that they are keenly aware of the vast rewards to be gained in this market. This is also apparent in the copy angle employed by many national advertisers in the press and on TV.

Staying with the visual media, a media planner has a wealth of teenage magazines in which to put over his sales messages.

It is a mistaken premise that the young men and women, who make up the nearly £1,000 million market, are too busy around juke boxes in eccentric coffee-houses, or jiving their way down the river on house-boats, to have time to read. They do read, and are avid buyers of their own publications.

Many media planners rate the magazines which cater for the well-known tastes of the teenage reader as the best advertising media of them all. Figures are on his side, for many of these publications can point to readerships of well over two, sometimes three millions.

The national press is now aware of the teenage phenomenon and their feature editorial coverage is taking on a younger look. The younger the look, the richer will be their share of the advertising that is directed at the new 'millionaire group'.

To sum up briefly, the struggle between advertising media for the teenagers' millions is getting underway. The money is there, the market is vulnerable, the media is gearing itself even more to reach it.

If advertisers and agencies can get down to understanding the teenage urges and itches their share of the market is assured.

So Newnes engineered a new title and aimed it straight at the teenage girl. This was *Honey*, born with the slogan 'Young, gay and get ahead!' (Twenty-eight years later, how that ingenuous description would be misconstrued!) It started slowly and its first ABC figure in the first half of 1961 was, in fact, a lowly 104,000. But the market took to it straight away and we feel that a secret of its success, in its early days in particular, was that it always followed the wise tactics of keeping ahead of its reader – but not too far. A magazine will always stay vibrant if its editorial content stays out in front, particularly with a fickle market like the teenager. Teenagers are always sensitive if they are talked down to editorially and can be equally switched off if they are being visibly educated by the editor. The success or failure of teenage magazines since 1960 has always been attended by the ability of the editorial to tune in to its readership and stay that bit ahead with never a hint of being patronising.

Honey's publicity at the time of its launch naturally exploited the exciting riches of the teenage market for the advertisers. By 1967 they were able to trumpet that the female 16–24 age group accounted for annual sales of £20 million on cosmetics, £48 million on coats, jackets and suits, £70 million on knitwear and £37 million on footwear. By the mid-1960s *Honey* boutiques were opened as shops-within-shops in provincial stores and the magazine was firmly settled into the media schedules of the big fashion and cosmetic advertisers. Audrey Slaughter had been appointed editor in 1961 and saw the circulation assume a satisfactory upward trend. By 1967 it had climbed fairly consistently to 210,000. Its eventual death in 1987, after one massive and disastrous editorial image change, saw its circulation at 118,000. One or two attempts were made by Newnes to exploit the *Honey* market further. *Honey's Bride Guide* was attempted in 1967 but this was not successful, nor was the abortive effort in 1969 to produce a twice-a-year fashion magazine under the banner of both *Honey* and *19* called *Choice*. The idea was to produce every summer and autumn a service magazine where all the advertisements would be created by the editorial department. Not surprisingly it never took off, perhaps because the advertising agencies were not too keen on this creative approach. So the interesting idea of providing a comprehensive fashion shopwindow for the under-24s died in childbirth. (The name *Choice* has since been resurrected and is currently being used as the name of a successful retirement magazine).

19 had also been launched in 1961 to exploit and build on the success of *Honey*. It achieved a quick success with its age group and was brightly edited, but it never enjoyed the advertising success of its pioneering sister magazine and lagged behind in circulation. However Newnes enjoyed holding two good cards in hand and dominated the older teenage market with the magazines. It is *19*, however, which has survived the course.

Other magazines that appeared in the 1960s to attract the teenager were D C Thomson's *Jackie* in 1964, *FAB* also in 1964, *Petticoat*, *Hers* and *Annabel* in 1966 and *Intro* in 1967. *Jackie* is still extant today but is only selling some 220,000 every week, about one-third of its sale in the late 1970s. It is really a teenage comic with a constant emphasis on pop stars, spots and sanitary towels but it is brightly and professionally produced and has a loyal following amongst the teeny-boppers. *Annabel* is also published by D C Thomson and in a way was their answer to *She*. It is a large format magazine which has always enjoyed a modest success. Since it came out in 1966 its circulation has reduced to 142,000 and in typical D C Thomson style it limits the amount of advertising it wants to carry and keeps a comparatively low profile in the business. In 1978 the circulation reached 272,000.

The mid-1960s was the time of the teenager, led and exemplified by the birth of the Beatles in Liverpool. The whole exciting world of rock and the other new sounds caught and fired the imagination of a generation. They found their new heroes and their own style – in music, clothes, by dropping out, 'doing their own thing', and other bromides of the age. Despite the many attempts, chiefly by IPC, to cash in and exploit this whole new excitement, the string of new titles that were hurried out from the publishing houses did not really ring the bell. Perhaps, unlike the entrepreneurial streak shown by so many of the young generation, the magazines were basically being produced – or at least masterminded and financed – by the older generation.

Back in the late 1950s the three teenage weekly magazines that together formed a market were *Valentine*, which had reached 500,000, *Marilyn* and *Roxy*, both selling 400,000. They were all strong on fiction but could not survive the generation gap. *Marilyn* slid to an ignominious death in 1965 with a deathbed circulation of 108,000; *Roxy* had already gone in 1963 at 115,000. *Valentine* survived for another decade but with a consistently and dramatically falling circulation figure. *Marty* lasted three years from 1960 to 1962, starting at over 400,000 but dying at 159,000, and *Mirabelle* had started in the mid-1950s with a weekly half-million sale which also steadily petered out all through the 1960s.

The point should be made that the constant movement and changes in the comic-strip end of the teenage market is geared up to replacement – so that the same basic formula is republished with different, updated names. This is a continuously profitable operation as the production costs are low and the editorial formula is virtually the same. As soon as a minimum circulation is reached it is time to pack up the title, regenerate it and bring it out again under a new name.

Petticoat was launched as a weekly by Fleetway in 1966 for two reasons. First, it was intended to take some of the advertising pressure off *Honey*, now really entrenched as the teenage monthly. Second, it was hoped that *Petticoat* would become established as the teenage girls' weekly, succeeding where the others were failing. It was to have a strong emphasis on fashion and beauty, rather than the shopgirl fiction of the genre. The first editor was Audrey Slaughter, hotfoot from *Honey*. *Petticoat* achieved a first sales figure of 212,000 which would have been strong enough for a monthly but was puny for a weekly. Within eight months of its launch it was given a kind of skin-graft with the inclusion of *Boyfriend* and *Trend*, two failed *News Group International* magazines. Maggie Goodman became editor, later to be followed by IPC's new star Terry Hornett. In its time the magazine was absorbed into *Hi!* which in turn was merged into *OK*. So, no British publisher was able to crack the dilemma of filling the weekly gap between the teenage 'comic' and the full-blown women's weekly service magazine, even in such a teenage-orientated decade as the 1960s.

The year 1960 saw the launch of *Flair* which was a Newnes 'me-too' publication. Newnes saw that *Vanity Fair*, National Magazine's very successful middle-market fashion magazine, was still on the crest of the wave. The art of 'me-tooing' is to jump on the bandwagon at the right time. If you are too early that market can be overloaded too soon. If you leave it too late, you help to kill the goose before she's finished laying. *Flair* was the perfect example of a 'me-too' and the two magazines were almost mirror reflections of each other. But, alas, Newnes had missed the golden years of the 1950s when *Vanity Fair* was waxing fat. Although both magazines were enjoying a fruitful advertising market in the first half of the 1960s the steam began to go out of them from about 1965. By 1970 they were both in a lot of trouble; both publishers probably felt that the one would prosper if only the other would do the decent thing and fade away. But this is never the case. When we examine the 1970s in the next chapter we will see how both magazines shared the same fate at almost the same time.

The glossies

Another launch with a short and unhappy life was *Fashion*, which Fleetway brought out in March 1968. This had very high aspirations because it was going to be IPC's own stake in the seemingly prosperous world of the glossy fashion magazines. The market was dominated by *Vogue*, *Queen* and *Harper's Bazaar* and although IPC's attempted entry was brave, all the wisdom of hindsight suggests that it was doomed to failure from its conception.

The *haute couture* fashion market was well served by its existing trio of magazines, even if their total circulation at the end of the 1960s only amounted to about 150,000. But each of the magazines had a positive and distinct personality and its own *élite* following. They attracted their own individual types of advertising, and there simply was not room for a fourth magazine in this esoteric zone where *Fashion* would have had to destroy an existing title in order to establish itself.

Having said this, thanks to aggressive advertising selling and the excess of advertising being channelled through *Vogue*, *Fashion* reached all its advertising targets during its first six months. But advertisement departments need circulation figures and it was here that the project fell down. The title just did not attract the buyers it needed, never selling more than about 70,000.

The first editor of *Fashion* was Ailsa Garland, a journalist of wide experience. Fleetway put a lot of power behind the launch, and were prepared to get heavily involved in the necessary and expensive merchandising and promotion operations that advertisers need in this market. This involves a complicated tie-in with stores and shops all over the country, together with a fairly lavish expenditure on show cards, window displays etc.

However, the circulation of *Fashion* never took off. The editorial and advertising departments were poles apart in their opinions as to the magazine's real intentions. It was never a beautiful magazine and never looked as though it was going to become a real 'glossy'. It would be true to say that it lacked style, never a criticism of its rivals whatever their individual vicissitudes over the years. Ailsa Garland was replaced after a year by Joyce Hopkirk, and Willie Landels and Jennifer Hocking were recruited from *Queen* magazine as art director and fashion editor. But the formula was hopeless and the end inevitable: *Fashion* was closed in the following year, 1969. It is a sad story to relate because the fashion advertising business would have welcomed a really successful competitor to *Vogue* – it is always an unpopular situation when one magazine can dominate an advertising market, since that magazine can afford to become arrogant and expensive. But Fleetway made a massive misjudgement of the number of readers who could have been lured away from the existing titles, or the new sort of reader they could create. *Fashion* was merged into *Flair*.

We can end our review of the 1960s on a more buoyant note by looking at the birth and successful upbringing of two new magazines that blazed a brilliant orbit around the existing market. These were two Thomson titles, *Family Circle* and *Living*, which were to create their formidable circulation patterns by a whole new sales life-style.

Family Circle has a rather mixed pedigree. It owes much to the amalgamation of two supermarket publications from the early 1960s, *Trio* and *Family*. The latter was in fact a quarterly, owned and distributed by Sainsburys. It was printed gravure by Odhams and for sixpence offered a surprisingly high standard. Although food and shopping were naturally its mainstream editorial, it also acted as a full-time women's magazine with all the usual 'departments' of holidays, letters, knitting, problems, fiction, competitions, etc. Thomsons entered the arena by a joint-ownership of *Family Circle* with Cowles Communications Inc. in the USA, who were already publishing the title there as a supermarket magazine. Thomsons were later to buy themselves out of the original arrangement in order to own the magazine completely in the UK.

The launch of *Family Circle* in 1964 is significant for two reasons. It was the first breakthrough for an 'outside' publisher in successfully challenging the IPC monopoly and, more importantly perhaps, Thomson developed an entirely new method of distribution. Pursuing the outlets pioneered by *Family* and *Trio*, and in line with its American namesake, the magazine eschewed the traditional newsagents and wholesalers and was available to the housewife only through the supermarkets and Woolworths. Thus they were able to achieve an immediate circulation of nearly 750,000 which established the magazine instantly as the highest-selling women's monthly. It has to be said, although Thomsons would and do argue otherwise, that given 'normal' distribution the magazine would probably only have sold about 300,000 copies and today the circulation would probably still be around that figure. But Thomson discovered a publisher's Valhallah and were awarded with instant and long-lasting success. In retrospect the mind can only boggle that such a strong and obvious form of outlet was left virgin for so long. Whereas the bookstalls of the nation bulge with every conceivable type of magazine, jostling for good display and attention, nearly every supermarket in the land carries *Family Circle* and its later partner, *Living*, at the checkout point.

The grocers could not lose. Thomson offered them attractive terms, on a sale or return basis, and although initially Sainsbury could or would not accept *Family Circle* because of their own title, *Family*, they were soon convinced of the folly of their ways and merged their journal into Thomsons, with the added reward of special Sainsbury supplements.

Family Circle has been an unqualified success since its launch. It has effectively reached its target audience of the young housewife and its editorial pattern is perfect for the reader involvement. About a third of the editorial is devoted to food, which in turn is obviously attractive to the supermarkets. Its circulation has been over the million, although some hefty cover price rises in the later 1970s had their effect on the figures. Perhaps the readers are particularly price conscious – after they have tottered round the supermarket shelves, noting the constant level of price increases on grocery products, by the time they reach the checkout to find the cost of *Family Circle* has also gone up again, this is probably the last straw.

Thomsons have never felt the need to woo the normal news trade channels to supplement their circulation, and, indeed, it would be interesting to see the trade's reactions were they to be offered distribution of *Family Circle* and *Living* as an extra to the grocery outlets. Maybe the grocers would react against their exclusive line being eroded by W H Smith. It would seem a fair bet, anyway, that the magazines will stay securely in their pleasant monopolistic situation.

Naturally, other publishers have caught the scent of success in supermarket selling and some have certainly tried to emulate Thomsons' successful entry. In the USA supermarket shelves are the main outlet for magazine sales (apart of course from subscription sales). Supermarket sales in the UK are still sporadic although ASDA and Tesco by no means eschew the news counters. It is still a sensitive and delicate situation between publishers, wholesalers and retailers, a situation we discuss later.

Living was launched in 1967 and although its emphasis on leisure has limited its wider circulation, particularly alongside its sister publication, it has always been a steady, middle-of-the-road seller and has settled down at around 330,000. Thomsons certainly hold two good trump cards in their hand. *Living* was probably brought out to create its own competition to *Family Circle* and by the formation of another title must surely have achieved that aim. *Living* was revamped in 1985 and was priced higher than its sibling. Its editorial changes were to reflect its move 'up market' so that the two publications would represent two different markets for advertisers and readers.

Odhams, in 1968, made another attempt to establish a new title – *Woman Bride & Home*. Condé Nast has been successfully building up their magazine *Brides* during the decade as a bi-monthly glossy for engaged and well-heeled girls. Odhams thought they saw the opportunity for a 'me-too' publication but with a much broader target of *Woman*-type readers. It was launched to be brought out six times a year, as the market is limited by the amount of advertising available. Frequency is an important factor in these rather more esoteric markets as there is little point in publishing monthly and losing in the other six months all the profits you can make in the good six months. But, by and large, the public are not happy with infrequent or eccentric publishing dates. They know where they are with monthlies and weeklies and their memories – and purchasing pattern – can become lazy when there is too long an interval between issues.

Odhams, however, must have been tempted by the advertisement possibilities of the brides' market. In theory this would seem rich because it opens up all the usual home-making equipment that packs the pages of the home monthlies. But *Woman Bride & Home* never got up the aisle and the father soon gave the bride away by selling the magazine to Condé Nast, who absorbed it into *Brides*.

Two other titles must be included in this chapter: one a failure, one an immediate and long-term success. Early in the decade Fleetway produced a weekly called *Easy*. This was clearly tagged as the 'His and Hers Do-It-Yourself Magazine'. The early 1960s were the boom time of the do-it-yourself, home-handyman craze. It must have seemed logical to try to encompass the 'little woman' into its orbit. ('Together we concreted the garden path!') But it was a massive misjudgement because neither the little woman nor the little man wanted to know. He got on with do-it-yourself monthlies and all his trappings of electric drills and screw-drivers, and she got on with *Woman's Weekly* and her knitting. It was a failure as a title, and a similar sort of exercise was to be attempted a decade later with the National Magazine Company's *Womancraft*, although this was to be a women's magazine only.

The success to record, so that we can at least end this chapter on a constructive and optimistic note, owed nothing to the big publishing houses. In Redhill in Surrey, in an office over a shop, a husband and wife team of journalists put together a bi-monthly magazine called *Slimming*. Its concept was entirely genuine and workable and it was to go on to be one of the big successes of the 1970s. Although copied and ripped-off it has shrugged off all opposition. We will be examining the phenomenon in the next chapter.

So here was a decade that could hardly be described as backward in coming forward. The publishers attacked the public with everything they had – new titles, new ideas, a great deal of capital and a savage, razor-sharp sword when they had to commit *hara-kari*. They stood on their heads, walked backwards and did anything that would stimulate a profitable reaction from the fickle few million readers who were so frequently and irritatingly uninterested in – or sometimes even unaware of – the frantic efforts being made on their behalf by the publishers. But if the publishers thought that the 1960s were tough going it was probably as well for their nocturnal contentment that they were not blessed with the foresight to see that equally bad times were just round the corner.

5

THE SEVENTIES

There is no need to dwell at length on the problems that faced the nation in the early 1970s. Roaring inflation, the miners' strike and the fall of the Heath government, rising unemployment, the price freeze, the oil crisis, soaring world prices, decimalisation – these were the ingredients that hit the magazine publishers as hard as everybody else. The price of paper hit all-time records in the mid-1970s, increasing about two-and-a-half times between 1972 and 1977. The big publishers, buffeted on all sides by rising costs, were treated like other manufacturers by the Prices and Incomes Board, and found themselves constantly investigated when wishing to increase their cover prices and advertisement rates. And as the big publishing groups had to submit their profit reference levels as companies, rather than individual properties, they had the added worry of a magazine doing badly and needing the solace of a cover price rise but having that increase denied them because other titles in the group were profitable.

Perhaps the act of decimalisation on 15 February 1971 was some eventual help to publishers in that it broke the single coin syndrome and destroyed the value of the small change in one's pocket or handbag. Up to the time of decimalisation it was considered essential that the price of a magazine should be that of a single coin – a sixpence, a shilling, a florin or a half-crown. With the advent of the 'p' anything went. Magazine prices tend to move up by 10p a time and the glossies have now reached prices unthinkable by pre-1971 standards.

This was to be a decade of great pith and marrow for the publishers who, throwing all their weight against the bulwarks, achieved some outstanding successes and some dismal failures. Some greatly heralded launches never actually happened – they were to be aborted in the womb. One particular magazine was not only destined to become a sensational success (perhaps the most successful launch in the whole history of women's publishing) but it was also to shatter iconoclastically much of the old thinking of women's magazines and help to shape the patterns of the future.

The first major event of the decade has already been described – the merging of *Harper's Bazaar* into *Queen*, or the other way round. Perhaps our indecision in clearly deciding who was merged with whom is a positive indication of just how successful this merger was in both aesthetic and financial terms. All through this book we witness the cold shot-gun wedding when a title crashes to its doom and is rather cynically put inside a stable-mate to try to retain a vestige of its circulation or its advertisement power for the other publication. As you will see from Appendix I, this 'portmanteauing' has gone as far as a title being put into a title into a title into a title. But *Harpers & Queen* can boldly face the world as two successful entities which were fused together (admittedly for economic reasons) to create an eminently satisfactory whole.

Two early births in 1970 came from IPC who extended their dealings in the shopgirl fiction market with *Loving* in March and *Love Affair* in the autumn. These were both weeklies and settled down with a circulation in the 115,000–150,000 class. They joined IPC's existing *True* magazine which had a similar circulation, and were generally ranged against the Argus Press titles like *True Romances*, *True Story* and *Woman's Story*. In a modest way they seemed to fill a gap for the romance-hungry and the nine principal titles in this market gathered between them a readership of about seven million women. Those pipe-smoking doctor heroes in their tweeds and brogues were still much in demand. IPC, never one to neglect a good thing, brought out a monthly variation of the same product in 1977 and called it *New Love*. They aimed at a circulation in the 200,000 bracket, hoping to achieve it with the bribery of free combs and lockets adhering to the front covers.

Slimming & Family Nutrition began as the bright idea of two young, if impecunious, journalists – Tom and Audrey Eyton. They started their venture in 1969 with a one-room office, £2,000 capital and themselves as the total staff. Ten years later their company was employing 150 full-time staff, 250 group leaders, 400 *Slimming Magazine* Clubs and they owned a health hydro and a magazine distribution sideline. They sold out in 1979 to Argus Press for a reported £3.8 million. In 1969 there was no title on the market explicitly catering for the potentially huge slimmers' audience. Their magazine was run on ethical lines which bravely entailed the refusal of advertising contrary to their editorial standards. Their reputation subsequently prospered and the circulation reached a peak of 350,000 bi-monthly. This frequency was dictated by the limitation of the advertising market. The launch and success of *Slimming* must be considered one of the best pieces of private publishing enterprise in the post-war years.

Needless to say, the publishing business did not stand idly by and watch such success without putting its own feet into such a rich pond. A plethora of titles followed on the heels of *Slimming*. *Silhouette Slimmer* came out in 1975, *Successful Slimming* (from *Woman's Own*) in 1976, *Weight Watchers* in 1977 and *Slimming Naturally* in 1978. The editor of *Weight Watchers* was the ubiquitous Audrey Slaughter.

Cosmopolitan

The watershed year of post-war women's magazine publishing was 1972. This was the year of the launch of British *Cosmopolitan*, one of the outstandingly successful launches of all time. The whole story of *Cosmopolitan* is fascinating and dates back to the beginning of the century when it was first published in the USA as a fiction magazine. It was owned by William Randolph Hearst, who seemed to have a penchant for the name as his film company, for which Marion Davies starred, was called Cosmopolitan. The fiction and feature formula was not doing so well by the early 1960s and perhaps the magazine might have expired if the Hearst Corporation had not been approached in 1964 by Helen Gurley Brown. She had become an overnight celebrity with the publication of her book *Sex and the Single Girl* which became an immediate best-seller and was even made into a movie. Helen Gurley Brown envisaged a new type of women's magazine based on her philosophies from the book. She saw herself as the perennial elder sister from Little Rock, Arkansas, who could advise girls on how to get the best from their lives, how to improve themselves and how to live their own lives – and not through a man. The liberated *Cosmopolitan* girl archetype would be out to attract men, hold down a good job, make the best of herself, and, not least, improve her sex life.

Hearst saw a golden opportunity. Here was the brightest new

woman editor for years with all the success of her book behind her. To start a new magazine entailed great risks and capital and Hearst Magazines have never been one of the great innovators. They shrewdly decided to hand over the ailing *Cosmopolitan* to this enthusiastic and energetic editor and gave her a free hand. The effect of Helen Gurley Brown and her new-style editorial was sensational. The circulation at the end of the old editorial regime was only 600,000 but within seven years it had soared to 1,500,000 and by 1977 was to reach 2,500,000 with a lucrative cover price of $1.50. Another bold step taken, quite alien to the hearts of American publishers, was that subscriptions were to be virtually eschewed and the new *Cosmopolitan* was to become a bookstall magazine. Ever since the relaunch 93 per cent of the sales have been bookstall, a statistic unheard of in the USA for consumer magazines. A powerful new advertising medium was created; advertising poured into *Cosmopolitan* and every year showed substantial gains.

Cosmopolitan was obviously a golden nugget in the Hearst treasury and it was inevitable that the British subsidiary, the National Magazine Company, should publish their own version of this magazine. They have always been particularly skilful in translating American products for the British market, as they had proved with *Good Housekeeping* and *Harper's Bazaar*, but there were three basic problems to solve before deciding to go ahead with the launch. First, they needed to find an editor of the calibre and personality of Helen Gurley Brown who would successfully orientate the magazine for the British market. Second, the market was pretty sluggish in the early 1970s and they had to decide if there was room for yet another women's magazine in the younger part of the market, particularly as their own title in this sector, *Vanity Fair*, was sinking despite strenuous efforts to keep it afloat. Then there was the third and perhaps the biggest danger that the whole concept of the Cosmopolitan Girl was an American phenomenon who might not exist at all in this country. Would the British girl see herself in the same light, with the same potential as her American counterpart?

The National Magazine Company were satisfied that they had the right answers to these pertinent questions. They were lucky enough to acquire Joyce Hopkirk as editor, who at the time was the women's editor of the *Sun* newspaper. Highly ebullient and crisply professional, the choice was perfect as she was to be widely exposed to the media even before the launch and was patently successful in conveying the spirit of this new magazine. National Magazines calculated that the women's magazine market was currently static and would welcome the excitement and challenge of a new title. They felt confident that they would find their own Cosmopolitan Girl, even though she would inevitably be different from her American counterpart, both demographically and psychologically. The important factor was that her attitude of mind would be the same – and the ingredients that had made American *Cosmopolitan* so instantly successful would also appeal over here. The Cosmo Girl's interests would be identical – her job, men, travel, her body, her sex life, clothes, cosmetics, the arts. Home interests would be minimal and babies were definitely out. The magazine would be big on features and fiction and the features would be very frank and direct when dealing with sexual and social problems.

Cosmopolitan was launched in 1972 after an intensive and carefully constructed PR campaign which has to rank as the most all-embracing, totally effective ever waged by a new magazine. BBC2 started the ball rolling with a 'Man Alive' programme in December 1971 called Who's afraid of Helen Gurley Brown?, which forewarned the industry and the public about what was going to hit them and contained some incisive interviews. The programme was followed up later in the evening by a Joan Bakewell 'Late Night Line-Up' which featured Joyce Hopkirk as well as some dissenters. From that evening the publicity machine slid into gear and never looked back. All the public relations activity was considerably enlivened by the editorial decision to publish a photograph of a male nude in the second issue. The newspapers really took to this one and spread the story, strongly denied by Hopkirk, that the nude would be full frontal. Although the year was 1972 it seems unbelievable today in retrospect that even a full frontal nude could cause the storm that it did. There is no doubt that this excitement over the nude helped considerably to fuel the fires of excitement that surrounded *Cosmopolitan*'s debut.

One must also record that the brilliant television advertising campaign, produced by the new and vigorous agency Saatchi & Saatchi, contributed enormously to the success of the launch.

The print order of the first issue was 300,000 but this sold out on the first day. The second issue's print order, male nude and all, was stepped up to 450,000 which took just over two days to sell out. And the male nude was revealed – or perhaps was not revealed – as being a bit of a non-event. Not only was the model's knee discreetly raised to cover his full frontals, but even his navel was air-brushed out!

Even the National Magazine Company was taken pleasantly by surprise at the explosive success of their new product. The circulation rose over the half million mark for one or two issues during the summer of 1972 and plans had to be quickly made to transfer the printing from offset litho to photogravure. Advertisement rates were raised at the same time to reflect the bonanza of circulation. The first ABC figure for the six months of July–December 1972 was 352,000, which put *Cosmopolitan* majestically above all its competitors.

An interesting point about the launch of *Cosmopolitan* was that despite its meteoric rise in the spring and summer of 1972 the ABC circulations of most of its competitors also rose that year, proving that a seemingly static market can be stimulated by new competition which is not diffident about spending a lot of money on television advertising. It is true that the advent of *Cosmopolitan* undoubtedly hastened the death of *Nova*, *Flair* and *Vanity Fair* but these were all obsolescent titles anyway.

The successful launch of *Cosmopolitan* was to have an immediate effect on the rest of the market. The most instant reaction was the decision made by the National Magazine Company to close their monthly magazine *Vanity Fair*, which had been battling uphill for a few years and was running at a loss. Now that *Cosmopolitan* had arrived so triumphantly on the scene it was a logical step to cut off the source of mounting losses and the death of *Vanity Fair* was announced the month after *Cosmo*'s launch. The title and goodwill were sold to IPC who incorporated the title into *Honey*.

The editor of *Vanity Fair* at the time of its sale was Audrey Slaughter. She boldly decided to branch out on her own account and, with the help of most of her old editorial staff, established *Over 21* in May 1972. This brave and unusual move paid off and after a hazardous beginning her magazine found itself a small but positive section of the younger market. After a couple of years of independence the title was bought by Morgan Grampian as part of their expansionist plans.

The death of *Vanity Fair* also inevitably spelled the death of *Flair*, IPC's 'me-too'. This folded its tents and stole quietly away later in the year and the title was put, rather incongruously, into *Woman's Journal*.

The excitement generated by *Cosmopolitan*'s male nudes (in the USA Burt Reynolds had appeared wearing only a Havana cigar) prompted the appearance in both the USA and Britain of *Playgirl*. This featured gentlemen in full frontal portrayal but the fascination never became successful here. Another American magazine with strong British affiliations was *Viva*. This was published by Bob Guccione, of *Penthouse* fame, in 1974 but W H Smith refused to publish a magazine with such overt nudity and the magazine had died by 1978. Its owner blamed the failure on continual prejudicial treatment at the newstands but his lack of advertising acceptance must have been equally disastrous.

Another event which we have to trace back to the launch of *Cosmopolitan* is the final demise of *Nova* in 1975. Even if *Cosmopolitan* had never happened *Nova* would have died, as we discussed in the last chapter, but the overwhelming success of the newcomer into *Nova*'s own preserve must have accelerated the latter's departure.

Another major magazine launch appeared in 1972. This was IPC's monumental flop, *Candida*, launched in the autumn, a tragic enterprise in more ways than one. It was a weekly, the brainchild of Jean Twiddy, and was to be IPC's up-market version of their existing weeklies, not a thousand miles from the sort of thinking about the 'new woman' that had been behind *Nova*. But Jean Twiddy was taken seriously ill during the development period and, instead of postponing the project, IPC handed it over to Angela Wyatt, the hard-working, down-to-earth editor of *Woman & Home*. Interviewed several years later in *Campaign*, Wyatt said,

> When I came in they told me Jean was going to be away for seven weeks and I was asked to advise and assist. I hadn't a clue what the magazine was about. I kept thinking, well in another week or so Jean will be better and I will be able to ask her more about the magazine.

But, tragically, Jean Twiddy died of cancer. IPC still pressed ahead with the publication and when it appeared it survived for only eight expensive weeks. The circulation target was 350,000 but it is reputed to have fallen far short. It was priced at 2p more than the existing weeklies (quite significant then) but it had a soft, unglossy cover and did not seem to represent much value for money. Born without any excitement, it died the same way. Neither the reader nor the advertiser ever really knew what it was all about.

The first issue was really indistinguishable from some of its domestic contemporaries with a feature on cookers, a picture story on Margot

Fonteyn, some knitting, shopping, cooking and the other usual departments. It was, in truth, rather drab and literally colourless. It could not possibly stand up to its first leader page which opened grandly with a definition:

> *Candida*, a weekly publication for women, noted for the fact that none of its issues is quite like any of the others; an unpredictable diversion; a provoking entertainment; a necessary addition to civilised life. . . .

How glib and facile do the editorial and copywriters' phrases roll out, and how hard to deliver the goods! The editor went on to state:

> All things to some women most of the time, you might say. Apart from our title (chosen deliberately to reflect our individualistic intentions), what *is* going to make *Candida* different from other weekly women's magazines?
>
> Our readers, for a start. Most of them will be recruited from those whose tastes in magazine reading are not being met by other publications. (Is this you?)
>
> Our fiction, too. It is our intention to bring you the best adult fiction we can lay our hands on, whether it is brand new or not; we are not afraid of reprinting, to savour again something really good.
>
> What *Candida* will *not* have is a prediction for cosiness, romantic fiction, solemnity about sex, self-righteousness about women's lib, trendy page design [*sic*!] or an assumption that everyone is a swinging intellectual with life-style and income to match. We *shall* eschew the little woman syndrome – the promotion of the human female as the terrifyingly efficient home-centred hub of the family and nothing else.
>
> We are after a balanced view of the life and interests of today's women; the kind who are stimulating company, joyous, interested, vital, intelligent, impatient and individual. That's definitely you!
>
> Why *Candida*? Why not?

We quote the editorial at length because it illustrates how so many post-war magazines have been set up, built up and consequently destroyed by their sheer inability to reach the heights they have set for themselves. After such an introduction, the lady with her 8p in her hot little hand is waiting breathlessly for the goodies to be delivered. But once again she just got cooking with aubergines and a special offer of a Wedgwood Jasper vase.

The following year another attempt failed to get a foothold into this seemingly lucrative weekly market. Morgan Grampian, basically a 'business-to-business' house, launched *Eve* on Michaelmas Day 1973, with an initial print order of 500,000. It was aimed specifically at 'today's young woman' between 18 and 24 and the editor was an ex-IPC woman named Trudy Culross, herself 24. The initial announcement from Spotlight Publications, which is the consumer subsidiary of Morgan Grampian, made all the right noises:

> The target area represents a generation brought up almost entirely in the era of television and an age of peace and plenty. This is a generation which is modern, self-sufficient and above all, demanding. *Eve* is for them. It will have a fresh, young approach on all subjects under the sun . . . it will cover all aspects of life. It will contain fact and fiction, fashion and beauty, etc. all presented with panache, abounding vitality and a touch of spice.

A perfectly proper hypothesis was built up with *Eve* and the aim of one million readers seemed reasonably modest given that the cover price was only 8p. However, a backward look at some of the issues tells a rather familiar story. The editorial was not really up to it. The four IPC weeklies were saying much the same thing with more pages and more colour. *Cosmopolitan* had captured for itself a sizeable chunk of the valued 18–24 market and *Eve* simply was not as sensational as the new weekly needed – and would still need – to be, to break in and establish itself. The first issue sold 350,000 and the circulation levelled at about 160,000. It was not backed with sufficient publicity money to buy enough circulation during the critical early days. In the event it lasted for only 13 issues and represents yet another gravestone in the cemetery of women's weeklies.

A bright idea for a new magazine appeared in September 1972. This was *Looking Good*, a beauty magazine launched as a private enterprise by Penny Vincenzi, who had been the beauty editor of *Nova*. She saw the opportunity for a magazine entirely devoted to beauty which would be sold only through chemist shops – a sort of cosmetic *Family Circle*. There would seem to be a perfectly acceptable thesis here to sell at the point of sale. Unfortunately, Boots the Chemist liked the proposition but insisted that they had the sole rights of sale, an exclusive deal which would cut out the other chemist chains, the independents, Woolworths etc. It must have seemed a tempting proposition to Vincenzi, but it failed to work out because Boots seemed to lack interest in the publication and gave it very bad display. A weak distribution led to the inevitable death of the publication.

The following month saw the launch of another IPC young magazine, *Look Now*, which was to join *Honey* and *19* in dominating the teenage section. It marked an interesting development of the 'franchised editorial package', as the managing director, Terry Hornett, left IPC to set up his own Carlton Publishing. This was an editorial service company that leased itself back to IPC, who ran the publishing side and sold the advertising.

Four other teenage magazines that emerged during the 1970s were *Blue Jeans* from D C Thomson and *Mates*, *Pink* and *My Guy* from IPC. In addition, *Hi!* merged with *OK* during 1976 and was clumsily entitled *OK and HI!* Renamed *OK* in March 1977, it was killed off in 1978 when it was merged into *Fab 208*. Rather like so many of the children's comics the teenage market is so volatile and the character of the editorial so similar that it is somewhat superficial to attempt a detailed analysis of the magazines themselves. Suffice to say that they will continue to revolve and evolve as fast as the teenagers themselves with their violent jolts of mores and lifestyles at bewildering speed.

Another aftermath of *Cosmopolitan* was the introduction of *Spare Rib* in 1972. This, of course, is committed and unrelentingly 'women's lib' and is published and run by a dedicated group of women. By glossier standards the magazine is never far from the breadline but it has persevered over the years and has outlasted flashier contemporaries. No circulation figures are published, as it is not a member of the ABC and its figures do not appear in the National Readership Survey. To the outsider it appears rather drab and colourless, a bit like a political tract. The advertising is sparse and it is not the kind of magazine one could recommend for a jolly good read. Subjects dear to its heart are women's lib in all its forms. It is uncompromising stuff which obviously supplies a real, if rather esoteric, need to a minority audience, and has to be considered as part of the rich fabric of women's magazines.

Terry Hornett at Carlton Publishing attempted to gain a foothold in the more serious market sector of women's magazines when he published *Personal* in 1974. This was a cross between *Forum* and *Cosmopolitan*, being pocket-sized and exclusively devoted to readers' sex problems. Advertising was severely curtailed, being limited to the two inside covers and the outside back cover. However it made no impact at all on the audience it was after, who probably felt that *Forum* was already adequately filling this advisory role, and it did not stay around for very long.

Women's magazines had a singularly damp year in 1974. It was, in fact, intended to be a dramatically innovative year as three major launches from IPC had been planned for the spring. These were to be a February launch of a new weekly, rather tritely titled *First Lady*; a March launch of *Duo*, a young homemakers' magazine; and finally, the big expensive launch of a *She*-type publication called *Woman's World*. But 1974 was the year of the great political turmoil, with Mr Heath's unsuccessful confrontation with the miners and the fateful three-day week. There could not have been a worse period for the launch of three new magazines of such dimensions and IPC wisely 'postponed' the launches, although in truth they were cancelled completely. *First Lady* got to the first issue stage, although it was never distributed, and one is able to look back on it as an actual magazine, rather than a 'dummy'. Hindsight shows us that it was not a particularly exciting or original recipe and the rumours in the industry at the time were that the advertisers were not showing too much enthusiasm for the project. We feel that if published its life would not have been very long.

Duo was attempting to sail through particularly choppy waters. This was the very area where *House Beautiful* had failed in the 1960s and was the market chosen by Link House in November 1973 when they put out *Inhabit*. This was the young homemakers', the first-time buyers', the honeymooners' and the bedsitters' market. As we discovered earlier, experience seems to suggest that such readers rather seek the experience and knowledge of the old-established magazines like *Homes & Gardens* and *Ideal Home*. *Duo* was painlessly withdrawn before birth and *Inhabit* survived only into 1974, leaving the market once again devoid of a 'young homemakers' title.

Woman's World is the interesting one of the aborted trio because it was finally resurrected in 1977, but one suspects in a different form from that originally planned for it back in 1974. It is probably a particularly apt, if not strikingly original, title now because W H Smith have for a few years designated the whole of their shelves in their new-style, open-plan shops 'Woman's World', as distinct from Leisure Interests, General Interests and so on.

Another phenomenon that grew up in the 1970s was the introduction and continuing success of the give-away magazines. This was a brilliantly simple concept of magazines given away at railway stations and at strategic street corners to a specific target audience – the younger working girl. By a tactful and discreet selection, an army of

63

girls are able to hand out a weekly magazine to the sort of recipient who can respond to the employment advertising which is its main ingredient. Response is the absolute life-blood of these magazines and the publishers of the two successful London titles were sensible right from the start in employing the right type of 'giver-away' who could realise the importance of only handing the magazine to the correct target audience. There was an early shuffling for position among the publishers, with Haymarket Press dropping out very quickly and closing their title *West One*. This is more suitably an operation for the small entrepreneur rather than the larger established publisher. The two London titles which have survived the course are *Girl About Town* and *Ms London*. They have both been successful in attracting a considerably quantity of employment advertising in a buyers' market but not over-successful in filling their pages with blue-chip display advertisements. Although their editorial has improved over the years it cannot be considered to be of the same quality as the paid-for titles.

There is certainly room in a thriving metropolis for such give-aways and there is no reason why, having discovered and exploited their niche, they should not be around for a long time to come. A late entrant into the same part of the market was Gemini Publishing in 1978 when they brought out a 10p weekly tabloid called *Capital Girl*, expressly to exploit the classified employment market. They originally announced that the title of the paper would be *Cosmo Girl* but this was indignantly and legally squashed at great speed by the National Magazine Company. As *Capital Girl*, the paper only lasted a few issues despite some reasonably bright editorial pages. But the sales pattern must have been poor, certainly in the teeth of the give-away.

The mid-1970s saw the launch of two successful monthly titles. First was *Home & Freezer Digest*, published as a small page-size magazine at a low cover price. Backed by an intensive publicity campaign on television the magazine was an instant success and achieved a sale comfortably in the 300,000s. The formula was simple – a magazine aimed at the housewife who proudly owned a freezer, although a great deal of the editorial content was not directly concerned with the art of freezing but with the kitchen and the home generally.

The main point of interest about *Home & Freezer Digest* is the original construction of its ownership. A new company was formed called British European Associated Publishers Limited with 75 per cent of the equity owned by the giant Dutch publishing company VNU – the IPC of the Netherlands. The remaining 25 per cent was owned by

Geoffrey Perry, the erstwhile publisher of *Family Circle* and *Living*. In fact, although the magazine was intended to be sold both through the normal retail channels and the freezer shops (principally the Bejam chain) only a very small proportion of the considerable circulation was through the freezer outlets. At the end of 1978 Perry sold out his minority shareholdings to his Dutch partners.

The year 1976 saw the launch of *Parents*, published by a new company called Gemini Publishing, owned by Hugh O'Neill. *Parents* was a franchised magazine from *Eltern* in Germany and has been a reasonable success, although probably not as sensational as its publisher intended. *Parents* as a worldwide operation has an interesting history. It began in the USA and its overseas rights were sold to Germany where it is published by Gruhner & Jahr, the big printer/publisher. They have franchised it to France, Italy, the Netherlands, Brazil, Spain and South Africa with varying degrees of success and then in 1976 to Britain. A further development occurred in 1978 when Gruhner & Jahr bought out the American edition, so the offspring took over its own parent.

The autumn of 1976 saw the birth of another women's magazine that, in our opinion, was doomed to failure from the outset. This was *Prima*, backed by the BSR gramophone turntable company. It was a damp squib from the beginning and a study of its early issues only causes puzzlement. It had nothing to say and nothing new to add. The old formula of a bit of gardening, cooking, fashion and beauty with a superficial garnish of sex would probably have worked back in the 1950s, but simply had no personality in the 1970s.

The back end of 1977 saw the launch of an extremely specialised magazine, to put it mildly, called *De Luxe*. Coming from an independent source, it was a sort of punk glossy with a modest initial print order of 20,000. Published quarterly, it could hardly get onto the advertising schedules and its editorial content was unlikely to appeal strongly to those who could afford to pay the £1 cover price required. It was one of those publishing oddities which streak across the firmament from time to time. A similar oddity appeared in 1978 when Baron Bentinck, a young man with a brewing fortune, launched *Boulevard*.

The National Magazine Company, much more used to success (*She*, *Cosmopolitan*, *Harpers & Queen*, *Good Housekeeping*, etc) than failure nevertheless found themselves with the latter in 1977. This was *Womancraft* which they had purchased two or three years earlier and had backed with a lot of their undoubted know-how and energy. It was aimed at the woman reader with time on her hands who could be persuaded to take up a hobby or two. The canvas was vast – from replacing a washer to embroidery, from landscaping to puppet making. Probably the area was too big and it would have been preferable to specialise. After a respectable amount of publicity money had been spent the circulation reached 90,000. But advertising was hard to pick up on such a circulation when the basic theme is so diverse and the National Magazine Company decided to close the title. It was bought by IPC in July 1977 and merged into their own crafts magazine *Sewing & Knitting*. But it is interesting that a year later IPC reversed the takeover and rechristened their magazine *Womancraft with Sewing & Knitting*, making an attempt to broaden the magazine's appeal.

In 1977 IPC approached the market with two new launches. In the first instance they produced *Woman's World* in the spring, their attempt ot get away from the teenage market and their formidable domestic range and try to get alongside National Magazine's highly successful *Cosmopolitan* and *She*. After IPC's abortive attempt to launch the magazine in the black period of 1974 they sent it out into the world with a great deal of optimism and not a little money.

IPC's later launch, in the autumn of 1977, was a pocket-sized title called *Good Life*. This had nothing to do with self-help in suburbia despite the use of the name of the popular television series, it was simply a monthly version of IPC's highly popular *Woman's Weekly*, which fact was prominently displayed on the front cover. The reasoning that a percentage of one circulation will automatically buy another one, however closely linked, is spurious in our opinion and is confirmed by the failure of *TV Times* when they attempted a few years ago to do a similar exercise with their monthly *TV Life*. *Good Life* was launched with an ambitious print order of 500,000 backed by a rather ambivalent television campaign. It was a small magazine in two senses and limped along until it died in 1980 with a circulation as low as 190,000. It was 'merged' into *Woman and Home*.

The year 1978 saw the life and death, in rather sudden succession, of an attempt at the successful formulation of another woman's weekly. The endeavour was made by Marshall Cavendish, who for many years have enjoyed a remarkable success with their series of part-work magazines, an art form all of its own and outside the scope of this book. Marshall Cavendish decided that the time was right to branch out into regular, or conventional, publishing and set up a division called Marshall Cavendish Magazines Limited. Their first attempt was the weekly *Faces*, an attempt to emulate the highly successful *People* published in the USA by Time-Life. But America can support a huge number of famous personalities and *Faces* was launched positively as a women's magazine. This *per se* meant that sports stars were not of interest and the weekly pages would have to be fed, like a voracious monster, by the faces and stories of television stars, royalty and the dwindling band of the truly international jet-set. This was a narrow front on which to base 52 issues each year and *Faces* was never up to it. Admittedly the launch was attended by two disasters: first, the National Union of Journalists' members on the staff were involved in industrial action and the union SOGAT blacked the company, seriously affecting the distribution of the first four issues. Second, the very first front cover picture of Prince Andrew was the identical front cover chosen by *Woman's Realm*. Sales were sluggish from the beginning and due to the industrial action complete distribution of the earlier issues was not achieved. But the truth is that the magazine was simply not filling a market need and it would have needed sales of well over half a million before it could become attractive to advertisers. The circulation guarantee to advertisers was 300,000 and the circulation of the early issues was only running at about 150,000. *Faces* died after 13 issues.

Company, produced by National Magazines, was also born in 1978. This was a totally indigenous launch for National Magazine – in other words, it owed no origins to the Hearst Corporation's products. Unlike *Cosmopolitan*, it was not an import but was the brainchild of Maggie Goodman, *Cosmopolitan*'s deputy editor, and Joan Barrell, *Cosmopolitan*'s associate publisher. Although the new magazine was to be aimed generally at *Cosmopolitan* country, the 18–24 ABC1 women's market, *Company* was planned to have a very distinct editorial personality of its own. Its scope was to pick up the *Cosmopolitan* 'heavy users' (who wanted more of the editorial formula but were rationed by the monthly publishing frequency) but, more importantly, to discover and exploit their own readership.

As this was the first launch by National Magazines since the sensationally successful debut of *Cosmopolitan* in 1972, a great deal of advertiser and reader interest and expectation was occasioned by the launch. The pedigree of the company and the main editorial and business personnel assured the new magazine of an important reception. In the event the launch and the reader acceptability was successful and the first ABC figure was well over 300,000. The year 1978 was good for advertising and the first issue carried 104 paid pages to balance the 92 pages of editorial.

The younger end of the adult women's market is notoriously difficult and fickle and many new products have been launched into it since 1978. *Company* has weathered the choppy competitive waters well and has proved to be a formidable survivor with a loyal readership.

In 1979 the Australian Gary Bogard bought *The Tatler* and installed Tina Brown as editor. The circulation at this time was approximately 11,000 and Bogard was reputed to invest heavily in the magazine which he was to own for two and a half years. Also launched in the spring of 1979 was *Exchange Contracts*, published by Home & Law. It was and still remains a quarterly, and its unique selling proposition was an arrangement with the Law Society to give the magazine away free at the solicitor's office to the client who has just exchanged contracts on his or her house. The magazine has been successful and one cannot fault the thinking that this is a very judicious moment to publicise curtains, furniture and household equipment.

Other titles that were launched at the tail end of the decade were *Food* magazine by Perry Publications and *Home Improvements* from Gemini. Neither stayed the course. An abortion was *Panache*, announced by Charles Forte with Leslie Field as editor. This launch was postponed to the following spring but never happened.

The last two big magazine events of the 1970s were the sale of *Slimming Magazine* by the Eytons to Argus Press and the launch of Sir James Goldsmith's expensive flop *Now!*

This was all conventional stuff compared to the awesome 1980s waiting around the corner.

6

THE EIGHTIES

Students of the women's magazine business need to keep a clear head when examining the births, marriages and deaths of the 1980s – a particularly volatile decade full of surprises throughout Fleet Street. It's heady stuff for mere chroniclers but we have endeavoured to marshal our facts and figures in a straightforward narrative. The Biography at Appendix III records these launches, strangled deaths and other manipulations.

Home & Law, following their successful introduction of *Exchange Contracts*, produced in February 1980 the first issue of *Homecare* to be sold through the Texas Homecare shops. A curiosity called *Curious Woman* achieved only a single issue in the same month and IPC announced that their magazine *Homemaker* with a circulation at 78,000 would be relaunched as *New Homemaker*. This innovative thrust only lasted one year when the magazine was folded into *Practical Householder*. IPC also announced the launch of *Photo Secret Love* with an initial run of 380,000.

A more ambitious adventure was announced by Joe Scott-Clark, erstwhile publisher of *Over 21*, of a deal with Boots. They would produce a magazine called *Beauty & Skincare* to be given away in the chemists' shops. The controlled circulation was to be 500,000 and the frequency twice yearly. It had an unhappy life with the breathtaking announcement in November 1983 that the magazine was to go monthly the following spring with a £1 million advertising budget and a 'settle down' figure of 250,000. It went into liquidation two months later.

IPC went in for a spot of juggling during 1980. They closed *Pink* and merged it into *Mates*. They subsequently closed *Fab Hits* and merged it into *Oh Boy!* As *Fab Hits*, previously known as *Fab 208*, already contained the bones of *Boyfriend*, *Intro*, *Trend*, *Petticoat*, *Hi!* and *OK* the story begins to get complicated.

In September 1980 *Sheba* closed. This was a magazine for Arab women, edited by Min Hogg who was to go on to a grander life with the launch of *World of Interiors*. Newman Turner closed *Slimming Naturally*, which had been launched in 1978, for the excellent reasons that they had 'insufficient circulation and advertising'.

In 1981 the Co-op announced a give-away called *Superstore* to be given away twice a year and then quarterly the year after, and the Alders Group announced their in-store magazine to be called *Reflections*. *Home Improvements*, launched in 1979, proclaimed a new look and a change of frequency. They would now emerge six times a year instead of monthly and increase their price from 50p to 95p. Each issue would be planned on a particular theme and they would now be called *Home Improvement Guides*. The year was a notable one in Fleet Street for Rupert Murdoch purchased *The Times* and the *Sunday Times*, Tiny Rowland bought the *Observer* and the *Sunday Express* brought out their colour magazine in April. There was a futile attempt by *Free Weekender* to give away newspapers on a Friday evening.

The spring of 1981 saw IPC 'relaunch' their 1960 young magazine *Honey*. We have never believed in the efficacy of a relaunch, at least by just deciding that an ailing magazine needs a shot in the arm, when it usually requires a shot in the back. *Honey* was to begin five years of trouble ending with its death in 1986. The surgery in this case was quite severe. The magazine went perfect bound to match what it saw as its main competitors, *Cosmopolitan*, *Company* and *Over 21*. It was adorned with a new logo, a £150,000 promotional campaign with network TV and, most importantly, a new editor, Carol Sarler, who joined from the *Sunday Times*. April 1981 saw the launch of *Rio* from Link House with an initial print run of 260,000. It was Link House's attempt to break into the seemingly profitable young women's market, billed as the magazine for girls in the fast lane. By the end of the year the circulation was down to 80,000 or less and in May 1982 Link House sold the title to IPC who incorporated it into *Hers*.

Sir James Goldsmith, having paid out a lot of real cash to advertisers by not meeting his circulation rate base, closed *Now!* in April 1981. Argus Press announced the launch of *Working Mother* which would appear the following year. In the event, the title never appeared. IPC announced two new weeklies for girls called *Heartbeat* and *Dreamer*. Trust House Forté bought a 75 per cent stake in *Food Magazine* from Geoffrey Perry and promised a six-figure budget for a relaunch. A new teenage magazine called *Kicks* was launched in October, with a 50,000 print run for London later planned to extend nationally. It was aimed at both sexes. The year 1981 ended with IPC selling *Womancraft*, purchased from National Magazines in the 1970s, to *Fashioncraft* magazine.

The year 1982 was to be a busy one. Shirley Lowe resigned as editor of *Over 21* as she disagreed with new editorial policy. A stir among the younger titles was caused by the advance publicity for *Up Front* from Independent Magazines. The print order was to be 250,000, the target audience females aged 16–20 and Saatchi & Saatchi, who had been so successful in launching *Cosmopolitan* in 1972, were hired to spend £300,000 on the launch. By the autumn the launch was postponed to early 1983 but it never appeared.

IPC merged *Photo Secret Love*, launched 18 months before, into *Secret Love*, and IPC Consumer Industries Press published *Black Beauty & Hair*. This was not a revival of the Anna Sewell horse but an ambivalent title aimed at Britain's female black population. It was planned as a quarterly with an early print run of 80,000. By the end of 1987 that circulation was down to 18,000.

March 1982 saw the launch from IPC of one of the more successful titles of the decade. This was *Options*. IPC were immediately ambitious for their new title, a 'magazine about choice'. It was initially to be aimed at ABC1 women between 25 – 44 which, although only one-seventh of the total female population, was seen as precise target marketing. IPC said that it was to be positioned between *Cosmopolitan* and *Good Housekeeping* and spent £1 million on the launch with a print order of 390,000. After an initial hiccup with editors the magazine settled down to be a long-term success for IPC. Its circulation growth and readership figures have consistently been efficient and by 1987 the ABC figure was a satisfactory 236,000. The readership profile shows one-third of its women readers under the age of 24, and only 28 per cent in their original age catchment ambitions. Under the editorship of Sally O'Sullivan it has followed *Good Housekeeping*'s role as a lifestyle magazine.

Kim was launched in April 1982 – 'a great magazine for today's girl!' was the cover strapline. It was a weekly for the young end of the market with a free Duran Duran pull-out poster with the first issue. The same month saw the purchase of *The Tatler* by Condé Nast from Gary Bogard – a leap forward for this hitherto rather staid glossy house. Tina Brown moved with the magazine.

No purchase price was ever made public although Condé Nast was quoted as saying that Gary Bogard 'is going round with a big grin on his face.' The circulation at the time of Bogard's purchase was about 11,000 and with Brown as editor the ABC figure for July–December 1981 was 25,427. The claims were that it had grown to 34,000 when the Condé Nast buy-out took place. The circulation under the owners of *Vogue* had reached over 60,000 by 1987 and there was a metamorphosis in both the quality and the quantity of the advertising pages.

In the autumn of 1982 IPC relaunched *Woman's Realm*, giving it the full works – new young editor (Richard Barber, ex-*Woman's World* and *Look Now*) a £750,000 TV and national press campaign and a 'relaunch discount' of four advertisements for the price of three. Although this was a common enough discount for new titles it was a rare offering from existing magazines. The print order was lifted to an optimistic 775,000 and the editorial was described as majoring 'on food and cookery, with a generous helping of cookery pages.' The trade advertising thundered that '*Woman's Realm* will never be quite the same again! (The circulation in 1986 had levelled to 600,000 which maintained it as the weakest of the IPC weeklies.)

The 1980s were tough for *Woman's Realm*, which saw another change of editor (Judith Hall). The launch of *Prima* in 1986 was another blow and in the spring of 1987 IPC decided to join the 'blip publishing' scene. This meant taking a leaf out of *Prima*'s book and running many small, eye-catching features for quick reading. There were other revamping techniques and Hall announced that she was aiming at the 'Oxo mum', the happy homemaker 'who wanted a friendly magazine and good value for money.'

IPC also merged *Love Affair* into *Loving* during the busy year of 1982, and Trust House Forté purchased the remaining stake in *Food Magazine*. Home & Law launched the strangely-titled *Fiz* as a bi-monthly to be distributed through the Dorothy Perkins shops. This title had a chequered life and its 500,000 declared printed order was ambitious. Eventually, after a bit of stopping and starting, it fizzled out. *Hair Flair*, a monthly for young women, was launched by an entrepreneur, later to be sold to Redwood.

1983 was a steadier year and apart from the death of the aforementioned *Kim* saw two launches – one of some significance. The spring launch was *What Diet* from Aim Publications (yet another incursion into the weight area), which has always had a modest circulation. But the autumn saw Emap, who had tasted magic with their *Smash Hits*, launch *Just Seventeen* as a fortnightly. The first issue was, in fact, banded free to *Smash Hits*. The cover price was set at 45p and the launch was backed by £300,000 spent on television. The editorial mix of fashion, problems, pin-ups and pop music was aiming at a distribution of 300,000. Emap saw a gap to be filled between the young teenage market like *My Guy* and *Jackie* and the young adult titles like *Honey* and *19*. While *Just Seventeen* has never been overambitious in the amount of advertising pages they needed it has always been a circulation success. Together with *Smash Hits* it forms a formidable young stable. The circulation reached 115,000 after seven issues and by 1987 was showing 270,000 copies, having gone weekly in 1985.

'People Maintenance' became a buzz phrase in the mid-1980s and Stonehart Leisure Magazines purchased the rival *Health & Fitness*, closed it and launched *Fitness* with an investment of £500,000. The purchase was no doubt encouraged by a Mori Research poll which indicated that 70 per cent of women under the age of 35 were taking exercise. *Health & Fitness* was aiming at a settle-down circulation of 130,000. The early sales were most encouraging with print orders going to 245,000 copies. The magazine was later to be sold to Northern & Shell. It was in the early 1980s that *Cosmopolitan* started to band, twice every year, their successful *Zest*, totally devoted to the health of the female body. A plethora of keep fit and healthy food magazines abounded at this time, mostly with small esoteric circulations. Many were one-shots, quarterlies, or bi-monthlies. We note *Healthy Living, Sport & Fitness, Keep Fit, Slimmer, Bodypower, Health & Efficiency* (all those bouncing tennis players were still with us) *Here's Health, Balance, Lean Living* and *Work Out* – as well as the survivors *Slimming, Successful Slimming, Weight Watchers* and *What Diet*. Later there was to be *Green Cuisine* and a delayed attempt to launch the American magazine *Shape*. Needless to say all the women's magazines, weekly and monthly, considerably enlarged their editorial coverage of health and fitness during the decade – a logical editorial development as well as being a ploy to prevent the competitive growth of this magazine sub-culture.

The quick announced birth and the very sudden death of a new story title from IPC also happened in 1984. This was *True Love*, which was to be a merger of *True* and *Hers*. Two months after the merger announcement the whole thing was called off. *True Love* was not to be published after all and both the proposed merged titles were killed off. The cancellation of the launch of *True Love* was a result of a dispute between journalists and management over a pay claim. The management way out of the impasse was to close the new title.

In May 1984 Terry Hornett, who had supplied editorial material to IPC on a contract basis, announced that Carlton Publishing would henceforth be a separate publishing company and would publish *Options, Look Now* and *Woman's World*.

The autumn was lively for new launches. C F E Publishing launched *Traditional Homes*, a £1 glossy for the owners of older properties, with an eye on the six million pre-1919 homes in Britain. *Working Woman* was launched in October. Although destined to be a failure, it was introduced and received with much anticipation and a fair modicum of goodwill from the advertising business. *Working Woman* is an American title which started with a low circulation base of some 90,000 and pushed itself up to 700,000. The American owners met many British publishing companies, including all the big names, to interest them in the launch of a UK licensed edition. It met with no success until Audrey Slaughter, erstwhile editor, publisher and proprietor of a string of titles like *Honey, Vanity Fair, Over 21* and *Weight Watchers*, saw the potential and set up a private company with a capital of £600,000. The magazine was launched at a cover price of £1.30, at that time quite a premium price, and the editorial line was positive and unambivalent, focused entirely on the working world. To quote Audrey Slaughter:

> Women now use a job as a means of identity and economic independence. They were always apologetic about working but now their salaries are very crucial and it is important they don't feel apologetic. *Working Woman* will use successful women as role models. There will not be much emphasis on traditional subjects like fashion except in terms of working clothes and how to save time.

The settle-down circulation was to be 70,000 and, as a slight sideswipe, Slaughter commented that 'the magazine can appeal to the executive woman just as *Cosmo* appeals to the secretary trying to be a PA whose idea of success is still marrying successfully.'

A brisk trade and consumer campaign, the latter using prominent posters, gave the expectation of a new idea working well. The print run was upped to 87,000. The magazine, however, never really got to the heart of its intended audience. In the USA this is known as 'pink collar', those ambitious, almost predatory businesswomen to be seen clip-clopping determinedly up Fifth Avenue. Perhaps in this country the top level woman executives read *The Economist* (and perhaps *Vogue*) while the less than ambitious PAs have a wealth of magazines at their disposal. The magazine ran into financial difficulties, with its ABC figure in the first half of 1986 achieving 33,000 copies. In 1985 Hal Publications, the owners of the American magazine who had a 20 per cent stake in the title at its launch, promised a further £250,000. They pulled out the following year. A rescue was mounted in the spring of 1986 when a white knight, in the shape of Peter Cadbury, stepped in. Slaughter was to leave shortly after this purchase from the receivers and a tyro editor was put in her place. This was Pandora Wodehouse who announced that the magazine had been too strident and over-earnest in its tone. The intention was to move towards more general features. The agency hired to stimulate the new circulation interestingly resorted to physiographics and divided women into three broad groups: feminists, feminines (men-oriented), and females, a fluctuation between the two former groups. Then they looked at the strivers, traditionalists (content with themselves and their magazines) and latent strivers, a rather confused lot. The agency felt that the feminists and strivers were already readers of *Working Woman* while the feminines and traditionalists were not in this catchment area. This left them the latent strivers and non-readers of women's magazines. Peter Cadbury was supposedly investing £300,000 in the magazine – and his ideas were very far from Audrey Slaughter's concept. But he closed the magazine again in the autumn of 1986.

The story continued with the purchase of the title from Cadbury by Brian Haddleton of Preston Publications. The magazine did not survive the winter of 1986 amidst a barrage of resignations, threats from creditors and general confusion. The magazine was to fade away like the smile on the Cheshire cat.

October 1984 saw a more successful launch with the introduction of IPC's foodie glossy *A la Carte*. At £1.75 a copy, and a circulation target of 80,000, this was to be unashamedly top gourmet with excellent production facilities and editorial. Perhaps it is the sort of indulgent publishing one would have expected to see from a small entrepreneur rather than regimented by the vast overheads of IPC. Its circulation has never reached its initial target, and a great deal of promotion money has been spent, but it has maintained a respectable piece of the top end of the market. As such it has been more consistently successful than *Cooks Weekly*, launched also in the autumn of 1984, from Marshall Cavendish. An interesting launch because the first issue was distributed with the 7 November issue of the *TV Times* and in *Woman's Way* in Eire. Three and a half million copies were thus distributed, backed by a launch budget of a £250,000 national radio campaign. The second issue, through the news trade, had a print order of 600,000 and the weekly sales target for the first six months was a minimum of 250,000 copies. Cover price was 35p. The results were disappointing to Marshall Cavendish and as its circulation trod a downward path it was closed in May 1986. It was immediately to be reinstated by Robert Maxwell and sold in October 1986 to Northern & Shell.

The poor performance of *Cooks Weekly* while it was still in the hands of Marshall Cavendish (its July–December 1984 circulation was 190,000. It was 'relaunched' in May 1984 but saw gains whittled away) had discouraged BEAP (the British end of the Dutch publishing giant VNU) from launching *What's Cooking*. They had been interested in a market they saw as 500,000 but the comparative failure in their eyes of *Cooks Weekly* was not hopeful to yet another weekly and it was shrewdly abandoned. The apt simile used by a BEAP spokesman was that 'they would hold fire, even if it means egg on our faces.'

Marshall Cavendish were not yet finished with their ventures into conventional publishing and food magazines. In March 1986 they brought out *Taste*, definitely up-market and glossy. Although food was to be the main theme, Marshall Cavendish had ambitions to extend its coverage to 'taste' in the life-style sense, particularly travel and leisure. This was intended to reduce its dependence on food advertisers and extend their selling to advertising for cars, holidays and finance. Circulation ambition was 145,000 and frequency bi-monthly. Marshall Cavendish had positive desires to break into life-style publishing at this time. They saw *Good Housekeeping*, *House & Garden* and *Homes & Gardens* as 'bastions of lifestyle magazine publishing and unassailable' but forecast that a number of publishers would 'snipe at their heels.' But a sudden change of heart, occasioned by their new owners in Singapore, led them out of magazine publishing altogether. They sold *Taste* to BEAP, the frustrated owners of the would-be *What's Cooking*, who have allied it with their existing title *Home & Freezer Digest*.

Other events in 1984 were the launch of *Chic*, aimed at young black women. Initial print run was 30,000 copies and cover price 90p. The editorial policy was to cover 'the whole spectrum of hair care and beauty, as well as fashion, fitness and all the other facets which contribute to the total look of a sophisticated contemporary black person.' Main competitors were *Root* and *Black Beauty & Hair*. The latter publication went bi-monthly in 1985 and the publisher warned the newcomer that the main problem they would face would be distribution. '*Chic* will discover,' said Greg Jackson, 'as we have, that a lot of newsagents simply don't think that a magazine with a black person on the cover will sell.'

In December 1984 IPC merged their two young titles *My Guy* and *Oh Boy!* with effect from January 1985. Home & Law purchased from Emap *Wedding Day* and *Amour for Brides* from RAS Media Moves. The merged magazine would be a paid-for title (the first from Home & Law) and would be inevitably titled *Wedding Day incorporating Amour*. It would be positioned against *Brides*, Condé Nast's successful title.

The year 1985 was to be a battle for the female teenager. *Just Seventeen*, Emap's runaway success, announced that it was to go weekly from the spring. Two immediate contenders appeared. IPC launched *Mizz* with a £650,000 promotion. It was aimed at 17 and 18-year-old girls. IPC were excited at discovering this new source of readership. *Mizz*'s marketing controller Stephen Parnell stated: 'We are gearing up to a dynamic and ever-changing market. If I have my way launches are going to come fast and furious.' He went on to approve that *Just Seventeen* had gone weekly – 'they've proven that fortnightly is a first-class frequency and if I were its publisher I would not have meddled with it.' He also proclaimed that

> we have identified a whole new market. These women have become self-aware to the challenge of adulthood. Photo love stories are behind them but they're not ready for home-making, divorce and Greenham Common. It is among this age-group that we have found a widespread dissatisfaction with older and younger titles.

Presumably similar cerebral stirrings occurred up in Dundee as D C Thomson launched *Etcetra*, another fortnightly. Their target area was slightly older, the 18–24-year-old woman. Editorially it would focus on fashion, beauty and lifestyle features. It saw its competitors as *Company, 19, Honey* and *Look Now*. Print run of 400,000 copies, cover price

40p. Carlton Publishing reacted by investing £250,000 in their *Look Now* which they saw as being strongest in the early 20s' age group. Cover mounts would feature strongly in the teenage war with Carlton announcing cover mounts all through the autumn and winter of 1984. The first issue of *Etcetra* carried a free credit card holder. *Etcetra* was closed in early 1986, not having attained its publishers' expectations at getting a foothold in the younger adult market. D C Thomson were coy at revealing any more facts and figures except to say that they had not been selling as many copies as they wanted to . The sales were reported rarely to have risen above the 100,000 level. The insider trade feeling was that the magazine never really had its finger on the pulse. It was also rather dull.

The spring of 1985 saw a new title from IPC which was to prove to be an expensive failure. This was *In Store*, a catalogue-style magazine, not a million miles away from the Habitat catalogue. The print run was 350,000 and the promotion budget was a massive £1.3 million, a record sum at that time. The editorial was to consist of reviews and listings of home merchandise products, claimed to be a new concept in consumer publishing. According to IPC statements at the time, 'people are moving away from general to more specialised publications and there is no other magazine that specialises in the home.' That statement, coming from the publishers of *Ideal Home* and *Homes & Gardens*, was perplexing.

> There is an increasing tendency for people to set up home before they get married. The home is more of a leisure centre than it used to be and people spend more money on furnishings for their home than ever before. For this reason we feel there will be no problem in sustaining a monthly publication.

The title was to live for only 18 months when IPC announced that the magazine was 'uneconomic'. Its first ABC figure was 116,000 and for the first half of 1986 was 107,000. Their aim of reaching 700 advertising pages was not achieved by some 300 pages. This was palpably insufficient revenue to maintain the production of 900 pages of high quality colour editorial. The IPC requiem read:

> The magazine's narrow editorial base meant that although we were getting most of the major home interest accounts, we couldn't take in broader categories like cars and foods. One option we considered was to broaden

the editorial but then we would have been competing in a very crowded market.

The magazine was not closed, officially, but merged into *Ideal Home*. It would appear as a banded extra supplement, some 32 pages in size, for about a year before it disappeared as a separate identity.

Rupert Murdoch entered the British magazine market with his announcement that *Elle* would appear in the autumn. But he was to create a precedent by 'tasting' the magazine in two issues of the *Sunday Times* colour magazine in May and September. The power of the Murdoch press empire was a considerable stimulant in the generation of excitement in the newstrade and the advertising business. The fashion and beauty advertisers were, of course, only too familiar with the French edition and the magazine, in conjunction with Hachette, had been very successfully launched in the USA. The *Elle* pedigree was perfect. Joyce Hopkirk was the editorial director and her comment quoted in one of the newstrade weeklies was that

> features on women's orgasms are a bit *passé*. Women are no longer interested in very wordy, very anxious articles such as are offered in *Cosmopolitan* and *Company* with fashion thrown in. There's now a new breed of reader with no special magazine catering for them. This is where *Elle* will succeed. It is primarily a style magazine with words.

The magazine was destined to be successful as an editorial concept, with a historic international record and the massive resources of the Murdoch empire. One million pounds was assigned for the launch with national television promotion and plenty of supporting space in the *Times* and the *Sunday Times*. Six-sheet posters were up on the hoardings from 1 October to herald the coming of the magazine. The product was to be perfect bound and priced at £1: very competitive to the existing fashion glossies. The first six issues claimed an average net circulation of 230,000 copies and the early NRS figures claimed a 71 per cent ABC1 readership with 67 per cent under 35. The total readership figure was 630,000. There is no doubt that *Elle* has achieved a strong position in the market for up-market younger women. Its editorial style is distinctive, bright and informative.

Other smaller fry were being born in 1985. *Knit & Stitch* was launched by Ingrid Publishing, a modest attempt which was perhaps rather prescient about later magazine developments in 1986. Another newcomer was *Lipstick*, a new fashion magazine for younger women with fashion and beauty as its main theme, primarily intended for the model *manquée*. And Katherine Hamnett, the fashion designer, made headlines with her plans to launch *Tomorrow*, to be sold through her shops as well the newstrade. Her ambition to be a press baron was articulated strongly. As she said:

> I want to synthesise the things which seem important to me from fashion, art, music and news to tough investigative journalism and get them under cover. And I want to shock – there are some things happening in the world just now which threaten us all as well as providing top-level entertainment. I want to use my magazine to shout my mouth off about them.

But Hamnett pulled out at the very last minute – eight hours before going to press according to the editor, John May. She later appointed another editor, Nick Rosen. After one issue the magazine faded away.

May 1985 saw the appearance of *Country Living* from the National Magazine Company. This was announced as two issues in 1985 and more regular publishing later. The idea of *Country Living* came from the USA where Hearst, the parent organisation, had very successfully put the magazine on the market. Although the two editions were dramatically different in editorial style, the concepts were not too far apart: the explicit drift towards the country life or the country style. The magazine was directed at *how* people want to live rather than *where* they live. A pull back to traditional values, of country cooking, fresh produce, the environment and conservation. The magazine took off immediately with a sell-out of both the 1985 issues. Plans were made to go bi-monthly in 1986 but when Carlton decided that they would launch *Country Homes & Interiors* in the spring it prompted National Magazines to go monthly with the March 1986 issue. This was treated as a new launch and both titles settled down to a pattern of success – with *Country Living* selling about 130,000 copies and *Country Homes & Interiors* about 88,000.

Emap, flushed with the success of *Just Seventeen*, launched *Looks* in 1985. Basic target area age range was 15–22 and the editorial concentrated entirely on fashion, beauty and hair. The first pilot issue was given away with the 18 September issue of *Just Seventeen*, a tasting ploy which *Just Seventeen* had enjoyed on the back of *Smash Hits*. Dave Hepworth, the editorial director, predicted that *Look Now, Honey, 19* and *Over 21* 'will be running for cover!' £500,000 was earmarked for the launch and a settle-down figure of 150,000 was anticipated.

The autumn of 1985 saw the launch of *Woman's Review*, a monthly 'produced by women for women'. A 48-page cultural review, it was launched with a 40,000 print run and a media spend of £15,000. Its appearance coincided with the relaunch of *Spare Rib*, a redesigned cover and a sharper editorial package but with no dilution of the extreme feminist principles.

In February 1985 *Everywoman* had appeared. This was published by a woman's co-operative aiming to bridge the gap between the up-market glossies like *Cosmopolitan* and the committed feminism of *Spare Rib*. It was claimed to be the 'first monthly current affairs magazine produced by women for women' and 'would bring a new dimension to women's magazines. For example, we will be producing the first regular sports page dealing with women in sport.' Paging was 36, price 60p and the circulation aim 30,000.

Cachet was also launched in the autumn. This was a 'big woman, or large lady' title aimed at the four million British women size 16 or over. Fashion for the fuller figure predominated, with general interest features. *Cachet* came from an independent publisher with a launch budget of £120,000. It was to survive only one issue but it resurfaced a year later when it published three issues. Its problems stemmed from under-financing but the editorial idea was sound and workable. The title probably helped to obscure it from potential readers, but perhaps a more direct title approach would have offended. A similar venture followed in 1986 with the appearance of *Extra Special*. This was by-lined on the front cover 'Fashion & Flair for the Larger Woman'. It is significant that both attempts have come from smaller publishers rather than the giants which may suggest that the readers, large as they may be, prefer the mainstream publications.

A new entrant came into the women's magazines market in October 1985. This was Independent Television Publications, publishers of *TV Times*. (They had made an attempt earlier in the 1980s with *First Lady*, a quarterly produced in co-operation with a pharmaceutical wholesale company, Vestric. With a print run of 150,000 it survived for only one issue.) Their new venture was *Chat*, an unashamedly down-market tabloid newspaper format weekly selling at 18p with a print run of one million. It was aimed at the 25–45 age group in the C1, C2 and D demographic categories. With 32 pages half would be in full colour. The concept was put together with the assistance of the Axel Springer group in Germany and based on the style of the German magazine *Bild der Frau*. The intrusion of continental publishers was to be heard of again – and soon.

ITP stated that the reader of *Chat* would be a busy woman and the new publication would acknowledge the fact by giving her a great deal of advice and information each week in an easy-to-read manner. Features would include fashion, beauty, cookery, show business stories, news of particular interest to women and advice columns. The editor of *Mizz*, Lori Milcs, was seduced from IPC and the project was costed at £4 million. Her policy regarding advertising was unambivalent: 'we don't want posey ads, it won't be pretentious. It's going to be the perfect advertising environment for food, retail, cosmetics and toiletries. You can do a really hard sell in *Chat* if you want to.'

In the event the product was certainly undemanding of its readers. The initial circulation aim of one million was over-ambitious and the first issue was heavily criticised by media directors as a mess. But *Chat* survived and its ABC figure for the first half of 1987 was 584,000 copies.

Almost immediately D C Thomson, suspecting perhaps that *Chat* was really their country, announced that they would launch *Celebrity* in January 1986. It would be much more expensive than *Chat* with a cover price of 35p and a more modest initial print run of 500,000. It was to be aimed at both sexes aged 20–40 in the C1 and C2 socio-economic groups. *Celebrity* would run features on celebrities, pop, TV, cinema, sport and royalty. It would contain cartoons and much of the editorial would have a humorous slant. The dummy issue had a reminiscent look of the then defunct *Titbits* magazine.

Sandra was launched in October 1985, a 65p monthly from Germany totally devoted to knitting. IPC launched *Microwave Cookery* as a twice yearly and Southern Newspapers announced *Microwave Cook* as a 100,000 monthly.

Things were also stirring at International Thomson with the facelift of *Living*. It was sent strategically up market with a price rise to 60p, a 15 per cent increase in page size and more colour. The accent was to be on more fashion and beauty and less babies and jam bottling. This was to differentiate the title from *Family Circle* whose circulation for January–June 1985 was 565,000 against *Living*'s 5 per cent drop to 411,000.

IPC ended 1985 with a bloody nose having to close their Emap-style music magazine *The Hit* after seven weekly issues but compensated (certainly not financially) by announcing that *A la Carte* would increase frequency from bi-monthly to ten issues a year.

The following year was not a star year for new launches, with the exception of the two country magazines in the spring and a sensational and surprise success in the autumn. As already recorded, this was the year of the closure of *Etcetra*, *Working Woman*, *In Store* and the buying and selling of *Cooks Weekly*.

A great deal of media excitement and attention was focused on the launch of Eddy Shah's *Today* on 4 March. A more low-key event was the launch of *Lean Living*, a bi-monthly appealing to 'more than three million known vegetarians or those with meat-free eating habits. *Lean Living* caters for the 18–35 female from all social levels.' The first issue carried the tempting free cover mounted gift of a lemon fruit and nut bar with a retail value of 39p. The cover price was £1. The print run was 50,000 but the editor, Joan Booth, said that this was merely testing the market and ultimately she would like to achieve a circulation close to 300,000. Coincidentally came *Veg*, a new glossy monthly, 'which is not just for vegetarians' priced at 85p. It took an intense interest in vegetables.

The saddest event of 1986 was the final death of IPC's *Honey*, merged into its sibling *19*. The magazine had considerably lost its way in the Carol Sarler period, gathering a hard feminist line which belied its history and its title. IPC, after the dismissal of Sarler, had tried to resuscitate it into its old fashion and beauty image but the newcomers on the scene, plus the old guard heavily dominated by *Cosmopolitan*, had taken the possibility of a rebirth away from reality. The circulation had taken an almost totally downward plod reaching a low of some 118,000 in 1985. But it had survived 26 years, the grandmother of the young titles.

Prima

If *Honey* was the saddest event for the women's magazine business, the happiest was the launch of *Prima* which was to dramatically and emphatically prove that the right product at the right time could once again scoop the pool. To call *Prima* a success is a massive understatement. It is one of those launches, like *Cosmopolitan* back in 1972, which not only creates its own success but has a remarkable impact on its market and conventional thinking.

Prima was launched by Gruhner & Jahr, the huge German publishing empire, publishers of *Stern*. *Prima* was already a major success in France, reaching a circulation of 1,400,000. It had been launched in Germany where it had quickly attained a circulation of 700,000. Their first move was to acquire their editor, Iris Burton of *Woman's Own*. Their aims and objectives were crystal clear from the beginning: a target audience of women aged 25–54, but aimed at areas of interest rather than specific socio-demographic groups. The editorial emphasis would be on practical ideas with how-to-do-it features and step-by-step guides. Recipes would figure strongly, designed to be cut out and kept, and fashion would be budget conscious. Areas to be covered would include beauty and exercise, homecrafts, knitting, gardening, pets, childcare, travel, DIY and cookery. There would be one very special extra value item in the paper pattern which would be inserted in every issue.

The magazine was launched with a circulation guarantee of 400,000 and backed with a £1.5 million advertising campaign devised by D'Arcy Masius Benton & Bowles. The advertising emphasised the practical approach to distinguish it from the gossip, horoscopes, and royal family approach of the other weeklies. As well as heavy use of television, there were full pages in the *Daily Mail* and the *Daily Express* on launch day, 30-second spots on all the 44 commercial radio stations and 2,500 poster sites throughout the country. The launch was a palpable hit with a complete sell-out and the second issue's run was increased to 650,000.

Advertising in the magazine was not regarded as the number one priority – *Prima* followed the pattern of testing set in other countries to get product acceptability and a loyalty among readers. The German publishing executive, Rolf Paltzer, even suggested that the company was content to wait seven years before seeing a return on their investment while they were consolidating their success.

And success it undoubtedly was, to be followed five months later with a doubling of the advertising rate and a doubling of the circulation guarantee to 800,000. The circulation was to reach one million – a record for a women's monthly in the UK sold on the bookstalls.

We shall examine the effect of *Prima* on the market, and more particularly on its competitors, in the next chapter.

In the meantime, down to publishing earth, smaller destinies were being arranged. A magazine was announced entitled *Boheme*, to be mailed direct to 25,000 people who had attended society balls over the last eighteen months. The year 1986 ended with the continuing mystery of the whereabouts of *Working Woman*, now providing speculation and high farce.

Redwood Publishing, established to involve itself in contract publishing with American Express and give-aways like *Intercity* and *Airport* (and later in the year the Marks & Spencer magazine) stepped lightly to one side to move into conventional publishing by acquiring *Hair Flair* from Casterbridge Publishing. This was seen as a logical move by Redwood but they stated that they intended to stay in contract publishing as well as moving into consumer titles.

IPC, while not firing back yet at *Prima*, launched a one shot in early 1987 called *Fashion Folio*, putting a foot gingerly into the deep waters of *Elle*, *Looks* and fashion glossies. It was aimed at ABC1 women with an 'understandable format explaining the season's looks and how to achieve them.' The print order was 90,000 and the cover price £1.25. IPC claimed a successful reception and repeated the formula in the autumn, announcing that *Folio* would become a monthly in the spring of 1988. (This was later abandoned when IPC announced that *Marie Claire* would arrive from France in the autumn of 1988 and *Folio* would be merged into it.)

The drift towards 'global publishing' continued with the international launch of *Caroline*, produced in the UK by British European Associated Publishers (BEAP) but launched simultaneously in Belgium, Luxemburg, France, Germany, Austria and Switzerland with a total print of 800,000. The English edition's print run was 80,000. The magazine is devoted to knitting and sells at 70p. Craven House Publishing announced that the American magazine *Shape*, dedicated to body maintenance, would launch here after an initial hiccup which delayed it six months.

The publishing world, and the advertising industry, were taken by surprise with the almost overnight launch of *Best* in August 1987. This was Gruhner & Jahr's weekly which had been hinted at for some time. It was considered rather unBritish, a bit unsporting and certainly very unconventional to launch in August when Britain is half-closed for the holidays. But on 12 August, a date more usually associated with the opening of the grouse shooting season, out came *Best*, backed with a £1.5 million television and press budget. Advertising in the magazine itself was almost eschewed – no one had had any time to buy or sell space. The editor was Iris Burton, who had stepped over from *Prima*, and the magazine was modelled on *Femme Actuelle*, Gruhner & Jahr's French title. The advertising sales director, Robert Benton, positioned the magazine by saying:

> One of the critical things about *Best* is the density. Our research showed that there is a measure of discontent with the weeklies and a feeling that they don't go far enough. Fun and entertainment are very important, but at the same time people want to be treated as grown-ups.

The actual notice of launch given to the news and advertising traders was a breathtaking two weeks. The 'goal posts' were positively moved, according to the pundits, by the speed of the launch, the accent on circulation rather than advertising, and the guarantee of a fixed cost per thousand, based on projected sales of 500,000. This was Panzer publishing – taking the enemy completely by surprise by the sheer nerve and rapidity of movement.

The magazine was Teutonically efficient and busy, with fashion, health, cooking, home entertaining, advice, hairstyles, diet, knitting – no royals, no gossip, no Joan Collins (all IPC's staple fare) and lots of short, sharp features. It was rather a weekly *Prima* without quite the craft element. The circulation rose quickly to one million copies, right alongside the IPC weeklies. Advertising was sparse in the early issues but Gruhner & Jahr were once again happy to play this patient waiting game – circulation first, then the advertising.

IPC were playing it cool, but if not stirred were certainly shaken by the German invasion. Susan D'Arcy, writing in *Campaign* (21 August 1987) suggested that xenophobia was probably the uppermost emotion at the south bank headquarters – more concerned with the fact that the invasion was foreign 'than the fact that *Best* was shaking up the meat and two veg approach in favour of a "nouvelle magazine" one.'

Best was not to *nouvelle* alone for long. Right on its heels came *Bella*, published by Bauer, Germany's biggest magazine publisher. They had, several years before, launched *Woman's World* in the USA, taking five years to achieve a circulation of 1.4 million. *Bella* was a British version of *Woman's World*, renamed for obvious reasons. *Bella*, too, was a sudden launch but was priced at only 29p, rather to the chagrin of the newstrade. It looked superficially like *Best*, with a similar sort of cover girl and lots of bright yellows, blues and reds on the cover. It, too, had easy knits, fashion, health, beauty, cooking and lots of snippets. But it carried real life drama ('She took revenge on a sex abuser') and royalty ('The taming of Princess Michael'). Why 'Bella'? Bauer actually publish a German weekly called Bella, but the UK magazine was more closely based on another of their German titles, Tina. The name Bella was chosen for the UK, Mr Weidenholtz from Bauer stated,

> because they wanted to get away from the plethora of titles in the UK called Woman's this and Woman's that, which all sounded the same. Bella was chosen as an all-purpose name with international credibility. It may be thought of as Italian but that doesn't bother me because the connotation is not negative.

Bella's sales started slowly with a technique of free mailing of the previous week's issues, adorned with a stapled wrapping bearing the statement: 'Bella. This is your free copy of last week's issue. Pick up this week's from your local newsagent now!' A possible snag to this technique was the startling similarity between one week's cover and the next.

Other activities were stirring in the autumn of 1987. The next actual launch was W. This was a fortnightly fashion newspaper, a full-colour tabloid aimed 'at people who care about and enjoy spending money on the latest fashion trends.' W is based on the American fashion gossip fortnightly and the British franchise was acquired by Kevin Kelly (founder of World of Interiors and Business) from Fairchild in New York. The launch price of W was £1 consisting of a minimum of 64 pages. The initial run was 60,000 with a settle-down forecast of 35,000–40,000.

The year 1987 ended with a host of speculative rumours and promised launches. The Spanish were to buy out Hello, based on their Hola, a photo journalism magazine – a sort of 'El Picture Post'. IPC threatened to resurrect the corpse of Nova, buried since 1975. The French were talking to IPC (after a failure to come to satisfactory terms with Associated Newspapers) about a British version of Marie Claire.

Second City, a Birmingham publisher, announced that at the end of the year they would publish Frills, 'a return to romantic frippery.' They said it would be an 'escape from the humdrum realities into a world of exotic perfumes, extravagant fashion and exciting undies.' Target audience was women between 20–40, cover price £1.50, with a

£100,000 promotional launch, including a cover mounted gift of perfume on the first issue. They also promised the novelty of regular features on skin care, beauty, make-up, hair and fashion as well as competitions and a celebrity interview.

But the biggest announcement was left to IPC. In the last week of January 1988, they would launch *Essentials*, a woman's monthly aimed at 20–44-year-old ABC1s and C2s. The biggest launch in IPC's history, it would be backed by a £2.5 million publicity budget. The first three issues would be supported by £1 million on network television. The theme would be 'practical' – a direct attack on the niche created by *Prima*. The cover price would be 85p, the initial print run 700,000 and 'guaranteed' sales of 500,000. *Essentials* would regularly carry 48 specially designed file pages, ready punched and perforated to put in a three-ring binder worth £1.75 which would be given away with the first issue. There would be index cards for cooking, knitting, sewing, health, beauty and 'snippets'. It was to be a full-frontal assault – the RAF was at last to take to the skies to repel the *Luftwaffe*.

And Emap were not to be left out in the cold as the publishing war hotted up. With a great flourish Emap Metro, publishers of *Just Seventeen* and *Looks*, announced the birth of their new fortnightly to be called *More!* Carefully targeted at the 15–30-year-olds, *More!* was thrown into the battle very directly against *Cosmopolitan*. Their launch brochure was explicit:

> The woman *More!* is aimed at is uneasy with the glossy monthlies, too old for *Just Seventeen* and she feels that the current crop of weeklies (even the new ones) are too 'mumsy'. *More!* will be snappy, easy to read, and topical. More importantly, all the editorial will be relevant to under thirty, independent women.

Statements from the circulation director that *More!* will be the magazine of the 1980s whereas *Cosmopolitan* was the magazine of the 1970s brought tart rejoinders from National Magazines.

More! would guarantee an average circulation of 225,000, sell advertising with a four for three launch offer and spend £1.6 million on publicity for the launch. The magazine was heavily researched and boasted one specific plus – a 12-page fashion guide of very buyable clothes from the high street. The branding and positioning of the magazine were extremely positive.

There were still two years of the 1980s left and the war for advertising, shelf-space and the loyalty of the reader was fiercer than at any time since the end of the Second World War. The race was on, the pace was hot and other media were going through similar transmogrifications in the eternal search for a share of the advertising cake and the public's attention.

7

LAUNCHING

As we have seen in previous chapters, the whirligig of magazine launches, with some startling failures and some exhilarating successes, hardly seems to be an exact science. Huge corporations can launch a dud, just as a small entrepreneur with a good concept can launch a success. There is no closed season for launching – the game is open to anyone.

In theory, a careful study of the past 30 years or so should teach and warn the prospective launcher all about the pitfalls. But, alas, as somebody said, the only people who profit from history are the historians. The past is littered with the wrecks of some abject failures which have been launched with plenty of money and goodwill. There is no common denominator in most of the failures – although even at the time one wondered in awe just why sensible men and women were putting their faith, and frequently their jobs, behind a particularly dodgy venture. The other lesson about the past is that it is not the present and certainly not the future. This banal truism is nevertheless worth expounding because there have been many instances of a magazine being launched which was distinctly old fashioned, full of tired old ideas and magazine clichés and plonked down into a market which already contained several such titles which had been there for years and were beginning to look careworn. Equally, it is purblind publishing to try to get too far ahead of current magazine moves which, instead of exciting the potential reader, merely confuses her. Needless to say, there have been many more instances of the former than the latter.

So the prospective launcher, like a general reviewing the battle situation, will first of all take a good look at what is already going on out there. There are about 130 magazines on the newsstands which are directed at women – and they are crowding each other off the bookshelves. The titles cover every nuance of women's life-styles, activities, working life, hobbies and other interests. There are magazines about dieting, keeping fit, sex, emotions, home and hearth, gardening, fashion and beauty, babies and motherhood, knitting and sewing, the country life, shopping and housekeeping, gossip . . . and many magazines that talk about all of these subjects and more. There are weeklies (a growing market again), monthlies, bi-monthlies, quarterlies and endless 'one shots'. Across the broad spectrum the socio-economic groups are catered for, from *Chat* to *Harpers & Queen*, and across the age structure, from teeny boppers and weeny boppers to distinguished and coiffeured matrons.

How on earth can this market, and all its advertisers, want new titles? How can new magazines find a niche to elbow themselves on to those crowded bookshelves? The answer, of course, is that this is the most volatile section of the vast industry of magazines. There are over 2,500 magazines currently being published and women's magazines account for only about 130. The ebb and flow of this section, as we have seen in our previous chapters, is enormous. Surprises are happening all the time. *Cosmopolitan* changed the face of younger women's magazines in the 1970s. *Prima* has made a sensational debut in the 1980s. The two magazines are poles apart. *Prima* is proving to be as cataclysmic on the market as *Cosmo* was in 1972. There will be look-alike *Primas* and *Prima* influences in existing titles. And around the corner, in the 1990s, will come another new magazine like a thunderbolt out of the blue to electrify the trade by its ability to read and understand a trend and, not only make itself a great success, but considerably influence the current editorial thinking. It is such dramatic and positive successes which over a period of time, rather than immediately, will destroy the competition, acting as a sort of weedkiller.

Even in the space of the ten years since our original book was published, we have had to eat some of our words, a particularly indigestible snack. We stated then (having reviewed and witnessed the recent deaths of *Faces*, *Candida*, *Eve* and *Capital Girl*, plus several old weekly relics which died in the 1950s and countless teenage comics), that 'no one will start a successful women's weekly magazine, at least in the foreseeable future.' The launch of *Best* has turned our prognostication to ashes in our loud mouths. Maybe our time qualification will be our excuse. But we exonerated ourselves by also stating 'There are other permutations of the launch which cannot be ruled out. The continental publishers, particularly the Germans, could become interested in the UK. Germany has at least two big consumer groups which may well begin to look at our market.' Were we particularly prescient or did Herr Gruhner rush a copy of our book excitedly to Herr Jahr? As we write, the French, the Spanish, the Americans and, perhaps, the Serbo-croats are all gathering around our bursting market to attract and seduce our 23 million women.

The women's publishing world has widened since 1978 and will go on widening. We have an attractive market to the foreigners. The Germans, in particular, need to keep on flexing their muscles in over-seas markets because their own is becoming static, almost overloaded with the sheer weight of titles. If you reach saturation at home you look outwards to the American and British markets, with their poten-tial for creating mass audiences for long printing runs. It is highly tempting and lucrative. The starry success of *Prima* and *Best*, and perhaps *Bella*, will serve to stimulate these continental ambitions and the onward march of global publishing is only just beginning.

It is at this stage that we would like to be able to say that the market itself, of avid women's magazine readers, is ever growing. But, despite the great comings and goings of titles, the fact is that the total circu-lation of women's monthlies fell by one million copies between 1977 and 1986. It is too early, at the time we write, to know what the effect of *Prima et al.* will be on the future of these statistics. The women's weekly market showed a 24 per cent drop in circulation in the same period – and again we have to await the effect on the figure by the subsequent launch of *Best* and *Bella*. So in those nine years the extant titles were all jostling hard for their share of a falling circulation market. It is at this juncture of reading this book that the launcher *manqué* may wish to throw away his copy, go down to a pleasant seaside town and open a kitchen accessory shop. But, as we have seen, there are always new suc-cesses, moderate or sensational, and in this chapter we wish to examine the tea-leaves.

In the original version of our book we were precocious enough (and subsequently fairly unpopular), to sectionalise the 18 launches of the 1970s into three categories: Good (including Sensational), Bad (including Disastrous) and Moderate Success. This was our rating:

Good (including Sensational)	Bad (including Disastrous)	Moderate Success
Cosmopolitan	Prima	Look Now
Company	Good Life	Parents
Slimming	Candida	
Home & Freezer Digest	First Lady	
Over 21	Woman's Choice	
Woman's World	Eve	
	Personal	
	Looking Good	
	Inhabit	
	Faces	

We were on fairly safe ground because all the Goods had started well and all the Bads, with one exception, had quickly died and were palpable flops. The one exception was *Good Life*, which sank to its death very soon afterwards in 1980. Our Goods section, with hindsight was generous about *Home & Freezer Digest* because although it started as a bright spark it has seen a circulation slide from 1977 of 356,000 down to 192,000 in 1986. *Over 21* had a similar slide from 128,000 to 81,000 in the same period. We were not, however, staking our reputations on the future performance of the magazines but on the success or failure of their launches, and all our Goods had good and sensible launches. The academically minded might argue that a magazine which failed to maintain its momentum was hardly a good launch, but many factors can work for or against a title in its commercial or editorial life.

It is interesting to have a look at a similar classification of 1980s' launches.

Very Good	Good	Bad
Options	Traditional Homes	Rio
Just Seventeen	A la Carte	Kim
Elle	Taste	Working Woman
Country Living	Chic	Etcetra
Country Homes	Chat	In Store
Looks	Celebrity	Cachet
Prima	Mizz	
Best	Bella	

The most significant thing is that our Goods and Very Goods (we have cheated by changing the categories slightly) are considerably more than the Bads. Over six Bads are all dead but our 15 Goods and Very Goods are very much alive. The reader will have the advantage of a much later time factor to see if we have been less than generous in our placing of some of the reasonably successful launches in the second column instead of the first. But it is heartening that the balance has shifted away from the flops to the successes and the one significant factor that comes through is that all the Goods and Very Goods have been successful because they have identified a need and created an editorial formula and environment to meet that need.

Lesson one in launching, or endeavouring to create a new magazine, is not to confuse need with condition. A condition is simply a state of being – a circumstantial existence – which in itself does not necessarily constitute a magazine audience of sufficient numbers or buying power to interest an advertiser. A need is a readership which actually wants something from a magazine such a readership being a market. Left-handed dwarves are a condition: they do not represent a need as such. One-legged lady hockey players, cross-eyed plumbers, hare-lipped butchers – these are all conditions and their simple condition does not make a need. But housewives, motorists, computer owners, golfers, yachtsmen, cyclists – these are needs. Collectively they are a market, ready to buy goods and services because of their common interest in their work or their hobby.

Similarly there is a danger in seeking a market in the current craze for labels. After the pundits divided us all up into socio-economic groups – class, coupled with age and geography – we were all divided into crude chunks of population. Then came the labels. The Sloane Rangers and the Yuppies have been the survivors – designer labels, if you will. But the competition to be classified followed fast and furious: the Old Fogeys, the Young Fogeys, the New Octavians, the neo-Georgians, the New Romantics, the New Unromantics, the Punks, the Post-Feminists, the Avant Guardians, etc. Everybody has a peer group but they mean little or nothing in identifying a magazine readership.

So what about age? It is obvious that a magazine aimed at the teenager will not, in general terms at least, interest a grandmother and vice versa. The National Readership Survey, the fount of all wisdom and statistics for all leading newspapers and magazines, can tell us the median age of all the titles on the Survey. The median age is the point where exactly half of a magazine's readers are younger and exactly half older. It is fascinating in our launching context to examine the table for July 1986–June 1987 because, possibly more than any other factor, it enables us to decide where a new title might fit into the market.

Title	Median Age (women readers)
Just Seventeen	17.5
Looks	18.3
19	19.8
Jackie	19.9
Look Now	21.9
Over 21	22.8
Elle	24.1
Company	24.4
Cosmopolitan	27.3
A la Carte	28.3
Options	29.3
Woman's World	31.3
Chat	31.5
Vogue	32.1
Argus Three	33.8
The Tatler	35.5
Woman	37.3
She	37.5
Woman's Own	37.8
Living	38.3
Ideal Home	38.9
Family Circle	39.1
Harpers & Queen	39.3
Country Living	39.5
Good Housekeeping	40.5
Annabel	42.5
House & Garden	43.3
Country Homes	43.6
Woman's Journal	44.8
Woman's Realm	47.9
Woman's Weekly	49.7
Woman & Home	50.3
My Weekly	51.6
People's Friend	58.6

It is a truism that a magazine's readers will gradually grow older with the magazine, a brand loyalty which may be good news for the circulation manager but not to the advertisement manager. In the broadest terms, the advertiser is keen to attract the 18–45 ABC1s, so a multitude of DE OAPs is not a sharp audience for the advertisment department.

So given the rather depressing facts that there are far too many titles in this multi-media world, that circulations as a whole have decreased, not increased, that the advertising cake does not expand simply to suit the rafts of new media appearing constantly on the horizon and that the instigation of new titles has to get so much right immediately in order to survive, where are the new launches likely to come from?

There can only be three answers to this question. First, the product has to discover some aspect of the feminine life-style which is going to carve a niche for itself in the market and persuade a couple of hundred thousand women to part with their £1 every month, or their 40p or so every week. Or, second, the product is going to be aimed directly at a particular sector and is going to be superior, or better value or more novel than any of the existing titles in that sector – and by sheer brilliance bombast itself on to the bookstalls. Third, the magazine might be an existing title in another country, and by 'global publishing' the international reputation of that title, or the reputation of the publisher or the simple fact that it is setting the pace overseas, can create the successful transference of that title. If it is launched simultaneously in other countries as well that may treble its advantage.

The sheer capital cost of a major launch today is hair-raising. We recognise that although launches will continue to get excessively expensive and extravagant publicity budgets will be employed to impress the trade and to bludgeon the consumer into buying and 'tasting' the product, there will be a counter-balance of small entrepreneur launches which may well slip modestly on to the market and succeed to the limits of the ambition of their proprietor. The newstrade will not warmly welcome such ventures because the cost of handling and displaying them will become increasingly exhorbitant. (The entrepreneur will probably have to resort to the fine art of subscription selling, a technique we will be discussing later.) But for the general purposes of this chapter we are assuming that the area of launching is national, playing for high stakes and the foothold on the market sought is big league, or at least modestly big.

97

Each year a major entrant on to the market is heralded with the fact that the launch publicity will be the biggest ever. Sometimes this is depressingly correct. *In Store* when it launched in 1985 spent £1.3 million on its publicity. This was unchallenged as the most expensive launch to date. And *Essentials*, the 1988 IPC launch, announced £2.5 million.

The major proportion of such budgets will go on television, as did *Bella*'s entry in the autumn of 1987 with a budget in the region of £3 million. Often other magazines in the same publishing group will run advertising and these are added, at rate card rates, to the total announced budget. A considerable amount of pre-launch publicity will take place in the newstrade press (there are four weekly titles) and the advertising and marketing magazines. These have proliferated over the years and their page rates are high. The cost of television time, and television production, is astronomic but the newstrade will certainly expect the electronic media to be used extensively if they are going to take the newcomer seriously. As all copies of all new magazines will be totally on a 'sale or return' basis the risk factor for publisher, wholesaler, retailer and distributor is, of course, in differing priorities – but the cost of simply handling large quantities of magazines (sold or unsold) is a major factor.

Perhaps their attitude can be understood when one considers the sheer jungle of the market and the very large sums of money expended on television by the many part-works which have been launched over the past few years. Their advertising technique is an exact science with a huge proportion of profligate budgets spent on the first two issues. They bulldoze their way onto the newsstands, brilliantly computed over the weeks on a law of diminishing returns. The newstrade understandably loves this great excess of television activity and the market has seen some very considerable successes, albeit some distressing and catastrophic failures.

Of course, a launch has to be examined from two perspectives. It may be from an existing successful publishing house which can carry all the costs and staff, apart from those immediately involved, in its existing structure. In other words, the ancillary departments like accounts and central production people, as well as the telephone exchange and the coffee machine, are already operative and can absorb the newcomer into their ranks. So the bigger publisher has merely to hire his editorial and advertisement staff and put down his publicity launch money. But the 'outside' man (or company) who

98

decides that he has a brilliant new concept for a magazine has to get his premises, his entire staff, his coffee machine and all his office machinery before he can set about the task of his launch. So, either way, success will not be bought cheaply.

But, of course, neither the size in itself of the parent company, nor its initial publicity budget, is a magic password to success. We have seen, in our short historical review, the emergence of successful titles from next to nothing. *Slimming*, with the Eyton's £2,000 start-up, is a classic to quote. But surely the last decade of the century will see the big action coming from the big titles – IPC, National Magazines, Condé Nast, D C Thomson, International Thomson, Argus, and the recently emergent Maxwell Magazines and Murdoch Magazines. Plus, of course, our friends on the continent.

Sheer size can be a problem as well as an advantage. IPC, for instance, is a conglomerate of three of the greatest old companies in the publishing business. When merged together they found themselves with a large number of sharply competitive titles covering all fields of the women's press. Some of the wide clashes have been eliminated but many remain. They include, of course, the satellite Carlton Publishing with *Options*, *Woman's World* and *Look Now*. *Woman* and *Woman's Own*, once the weekly flagships of Odhams Press and Newnes have long been shipmates on the south bank instead of being fiercely competitive. IPC now cover such a range of women's titles that they have to consider deeply before launching a new magazine which will oppose one of their current titles and qualify for a piece of the advertising take as well as threatening circulation. On the other hand, with so many titles they hold the advantage of launching their own competition just when the timing and the market suits them. National Magazines, with six aces in their hands, has a similar problem of duplicating one of their own successes, but managed to launch *Company* as a very explicit new product in the teeth of *Cosmopolitan*. And Condé Nast, who only publish high-quality glossies, may have to stagnate or widen their sphere of activity.

But do the big companies really and sincerely want to launch new magazines? Is it in their collective interest to go through the soul-shuddering, nail-biting exercise of launches which, if unsuccessful, would blow uncomfortable holes in their company profits? It would be convenient to think that the whole market is a cosy carve-up which would, or could, close ranks to any newcomer. But a glance at BRAD will demonstrate how fragmented the market is in reality. At the time

99

of writing IPC owned 25 titles, National Magazines five, D C Thomson nine, Thomsons three, Argus Press five, and 41 are published by independents. The big five companies are in a constant state of gentlemanly but fierce warfare, seeking the maximum input of advertising and readers. Like any other business the publishers can neither afford to stand still and let outsiders move in, nor to lose any initiative to each other.

Apart from the commercial manoeuvres of the big publishers and their various reasons for launching a new title, it would seem that magazines have always had an attraction for amateurs and dilettantes, rather as the world of show-biz has a fascination for the well-heeled 'angel'. Probably every journalist dreams of owning his own local paper or magazine and many a businessman, successful in his own field, picks up a copy of *Vogue*, *Woman* or *Cosmopolitan* and is mesmerised by the amount of advertising gracing the pages. It looks deceptively simple to out-glossy the glossies or just to produce a better version of *Ideal Home* or *Woman's Realm*. And there are, on the face of it, so few restrictions. Anybody can set up in business as a magazine publisher. You do not need a franchise or a licence. You do not need a printing works like a newspaper. You simply need to invent your title (which can't even be copyrighted), appoint your editor and off you go. The Londoner's Diary in the *Evening Standard* will 'write you up' because they seem to have a ghoulish interest in the follies of the amateur publisher. Its a free country – you're perfectly at liberty to make yourself bankrupt.

There seems little doubt that the first question which the publisher must answer is simply – *raison d'être*. Is the subject matter of the title really and genuinely new – reflecting some new aspect of human life or behaviour? Or is the proposed treatment of a more familiar subject or range of subjects going to be so superior to existing titles that readers of the other magazines will change loyalties and come over to you? If the answer is affirmative you can move on to the next square. And this is in big, black, block capitals: can you get the advertising? Because magazines have to live on their advertising revenue. No women's magazine makes a profit out of its cover price and, in our view, never will. Cover prices lag too far behind the proper price for them to clamber up in any thing like the foreseeable future. So your women's magazine is going to rely on its advertising potential. This, in turn, means that new launches are going to be class periodicals; in other words, they are going to specialise in some clearly defined area of human activity.

It will be tempting, therefore, for the new launch to be directed at certain areas. The 'home' as an all-embracing term is always one of the most obvious. A look through the pages of all the successful monthlies shows a seemingly unending wealth of colour advertising. Here is a very positive market segment of high quality goods which basically are too up market to appear on television or in most of the national dailies. Another area is young women, or teenagers, with the huge range of fashion and beauty products. And certainly these two subjects alone have been at the centre of the launches in the past decade. But they have also seen a few crash-dives: *Inhabit, Duo, House Beautiful, Eve, Vanity Fair* and *Flair* are examples which spring to mind.

There is another gratuitous piece of advice for the smaller launcher of new magazines. A mistake we have seen perpetrated again and again economising on the initial executive staff. Second-rate people will almost automatically make a second-rate magazine – although first-rate people will not of course *guarantee* a first-rate magazine. However, to hire second graders, in order to save on launching costs, is the direst false economy it is possible to make. Going out into the market and buying the top advertisement man in the field, and the very best editorial people, will pay off handsomely – assuming that the magazine has worth in the first place. There are two reasons for this. First, the staff will be professional and hard working and produce the best results. Second, their very presence on the masthead of the magazine will blatantly announce to the world that here is a magazine that really means business, is going to be properly run and is backed not only by the publisher's money but by the talents and professional future of certain well-known people.

Certainly the younger woman's market will be attractive to the launcher. We have seen how *Cosmopolitan* flashed its way on to the market in 1972, followed by its sibling *Company* seven years later. It is a tempting piece of the action if only because the younger reader has not formed a life-time reading allegiance to a particular magazine, is probably bursting to rebel against anything old or established and will appear, in her own image, smart and different by taking the newest magazine to her bosom. She also presents the advertiser with his most lucrative market in the wide fields of cosmetics, toiletries and other goods. She is by her nature a light TV viewer and therefore difficult to reach with more expensive and wasteful mass media. Now that girls are better educated, more affluent than ever before and marrying later in life, the whole new phenomenon of the 'independent woman' offers rich prizes to both publisher and advertiser. It is a proven fact that young women, particularly those without children, are heavy magazine buyers and readers. A childless woman in her early 20s will buy two or three times the number of magazines purchased by a woman of the same age and social class who has children. It is the classic marketing pattern of a high proportion of purchases being made by a minority of heavy users. This is why there will always be a strong duplication of titles around a particular part of the magazine market, because the heavy users cannot go on buying the same magazine more times than its frequency of publication. But the teenage area, both weeny and teeny, and the 18–24 age range is well covered by existing titles and is not limitless in its expansion, and the new publisher or the new magazine has to break into formidable competition.

We have already mentioned the myth and the difficulties of the relaunch. Not so prevalent these days as a decade or so ago, it is nevertheless a tempting tactic for the existing magazine which has run into trouble. Obviously the publisher with such a problem still retains one ace in his hand: he owns a title which is still evocative and will be recognised by a certain segment of the readership he still needs. He has a nucleus of regular and loyal customers, both as readers and advertisers. But both have been leaving him over the years, one as a result of the other. He can capitulate, bless the good times the title has given him over the years, and retire it gracefully while people still have fond memories. At the same time, he feels that the title is too good simply to throw away as he will probably then have to launch a completely virgin title on to the crowded market and spend a great deal of money making it familiar. The long-term advertisers will look on the new brainchild as something different and will by no means feel that they must transfer their expensive space from the old to the new, probably at a more excessive rate.

Why not instead decide that a facelift, a change of editor, a new format, some publicity and an injection of new ideas will be the simpler and cheaper course? At the most basic it saves the publisher having to dream up a new title, an exercise which is becoming almost an art form in itself. The word 'woman' has been through just about every permutation, sometimes more than once, and the word in itself on the front cover is no longer any passport to instant success. (It is interesting that the word does not appear on the front cover of any of the really successful magazines launched in the past couple of decades.) No, his old title can be turned to positive advantage, perhaps with a revise of the logo. (The publisher cannot, or certainly has never tried to emulate the current practice of the film producers by following up the blockbuster film with a second version with the figure 2 after the title. *Vanity Fair 2*, *Woman's World 4* is an interesting, if idle, conjecture.)

It would be good to record a single instance of a really successful example of a relaunched women's magazine in this country. There have, of course, been evolutions like *Queen* which over two or three years was slowly and deliberately moved by Jocelyn Stevens from a prim society journal to the signal success it was in the 1960s as a trendy, reflective and rather satirical mirror of the decade. But by no means did he try to do this overnight. And, of course, almost every women's magazine has changed with the times (there are exceptions!) but the pace has always been sensibly set not to startle the horses.

This is not to state that there have not been highly successful and interesting rejuvenations. *Woman's Journal* was given a relaunch in 1977 and trumpeted:

> a completely new and dynamic *Woman's Journal* will be appearing on our bookstalls on 21 February. The March issue will be entirely different from the *Woman's Journal* we all know. It is to be expanded into a broader based publication, still with an AB bias but with a strong appeal for the much wider audience provided by the CI readership group. The new *Woman's Journal* will editorially aim for the younger woman who is on her way up, either in her own right or through her husband.

The real success of the turnaround of *Woman's Journal* (which IPC had planned to close if the relaunch was a failure) came with the arrival of Laurie Purden, an ex-editor of *Good Housekeeping*. She has brought a flair and a style to the magazine which has given it a new thrust. But the magazine she has been editing so elegantly is not the marketeers' vision: as we have seen earlier in this chapter the median age in 1987 was 44.8 and the socio-economic profile is 64 per cent over 25 and 64 per cent C1, C2, DE. The salvation of *Woman's Journal* was heartening to the magazine business, proving that an editorial facelift, backed with professional management, has an important part to play in regenerating ailing titles.

She saw a similar injection of high-level electric energy when National Magazines brought in the highly experienced Joyce Hopkirk to take over the editorship. Time will tell how successful the treatment is in commercial terms but in editorial buzz and visual impact the facelift speaks for itself, Tina Brown's editorial metamorphosis of *The Tatler* is another example.

There is yet another factor in the publishers' never-ending search for new titles. It is possible to dip a toe in the water with a one-off issue and thereby test both trade and reader reaction to the title. This is quite expensive because the single edition is unlikely to be financially self-supporting (it will certainly have to be sale or return to the trade) and will have to be advertised. One-offs are not over welcome in the newstrade because of the excessive amount of handling involved when dealing with returns. There is no doubt that they give the editorial staff a genuine opportunity to flex their muscles over the idea and the publisher and circulation staff a reasonable assessment of the publication's possibilities. IPC experimented in 1974 with a 98-page one-off for *Woman's Own* called *Successful Slimming* which they later converted into a bi-monthly in this difficult sector of the market. Obviously a different set of values applies in assessing the one-off as against issue number one of a regular title, but it is likely that this kind of kite-flying will become a more prominent feature of publishing in the rest of the century. It represents a mini-launch at a fraction of the cost and risk attached to a real launch, and it is in the interest of all concerned that the number of expensive failures should be reduced.

It was in the 1980s when the one-off, or pilot issue, was emphatically introduced increasingly by the publishers. The horrific cost of a full-blooded, full frontal launch represents a real risk which the publishing industry began to get diffident about. It is a logical strategy, both from a reputation as well as a financial viewpoint, to put the elbow in the bath water to assess the temperature before the baby is popped in. 'Lower frequency' launches were *A la Carte*, launched as alternate months and *In Store* with ten issues. (Ten issues were prevalent in the 1950s and the 1960s for so-called 'monthly' magazines which wished to avoid the embarrassment of ludicrously badly supported January and August issues. Such a cop-out has slid out of fashion as the monthly magazine war has hotted up and the gap between the issues each side of the missing month is too long. You cannot afford a time gap in which your advertisers and your reading public may forget you in a very crowded market.)

Taste began with seven issues annually and *Elle* was positively blushing with natal nerves as the magazine was slowly exposed to the waiting readership. Not only did the first two issues appear as part of the *Sunday Times* colour magazine (the first one in May appeared only in the Southern edition), but when it was launched on the market as an entirely separate entity the first three issues were at six weekly intervals. IPC's *Folio* appeared as a one shot in the spring of 1987 and the intention was to turn it into a quarterly fashion magazine selling 75,000 copies. Heather Love, the publisher, was reported as saying that *Folio* was what the editor Glenda Bailey and she had envisaged turning *Honey* into before the enforced closure of that magazine. By all accounts *Folio* was doing well and the decision was taken by IPC, presumably happy with the bookstall sales and advertising reaction to their sporadic issues, to go monthly from the spring of 1988. Events moved faster, however, and *Folio* was destined to turn into a supplement called *Fashion Folio* in the emergent *Marie Claire*. It would have been interesting lineage for poor old abused *Honey*, which had begun its life in 1960 as such a trendsetter.

Another outstanding sample of the softly softly launch technique was *Country Living*. The American version had been startlingly successful in circulation building and had moved from one shot, through quarterly and bi-monthly to monthly. This was now almost an established technique with the Hearst Corporation who had followed the system with *Colonial Homes*. National Magazines, a wholly owned subsidiary of Hearst, decided to test this hitherto undeveloped market with the British version of *Country Living*. Two issues were piloted, the first in May 1986 and the second in November. The intention was made clear right at the outset in presentations to the newstrade and the advertising business that 1987 would see a continuation of publishing with a frequency to be decided later. The first two issues were sell-out successes with solid support from advertisers. A decision was made to go bi-monthly in 1987 from the March issue but this was later rescinded to monthly publication from the same month. That decision was based on commercial foresight but not unconnected with the announced advent of *Country Homes & Interiors* from Carlton Publishing also to be published in the spring. The two launches are interesting to compare because the National Magazine title spent not one publicity penny on their two pilot issues and a very modest campaign on the spring launch, whereas Carlton used television and the press quite extensively for their early issues. With a modest price difference (Carlton £1.10 to National Magazine's £1) the circulation gap has always been some 30,000 copies to the advantage of *Country Living*.

Frequency of publication is another launching decision. The two most obvious choices are weekly and monthly and all the mainstream titles take one course or the other. But there are exceptions. The slimming magazines are bi-monthly. The main reason is the paucity of advertising to fill 12 issues a year, making it preferable to publish six fatter and more profitable issues each year than to stretch resources more thinly 12 times. And sometimes frequency is changed in midstream. *Queen* magazine, back in the early 1960s while still owned by Jocelyn Stevens, switched from fortnightly publication to weekly. It overreached itself in endeavouring to retain the same advertising and circulation momentum and scuttled back to the more convenient frequency after just one year. Condé Nast's *Vogue*, and *Harpers & Queen* in the early period after its launch, published 16 issues a year, with the double months being March, April, September and October. Again, this was a strain on the advertisement department and the circulation manager, as well as creating a confusion in the minds of the regular buyers. It is, therefore, best to find your most profitable frequency and stick to it. *Private Eye*, for instance, has stuck to its last ever since its first issue as a fortnightly. This is perfect for such a title with its iconoclastic topicality – weekly would be rather tiresome to the buyer.

Just Seventeen started life as a fortnightly in September 1983 and went weekly in May 1985. This was after Emap's assessment of the capabilities of the title which was simply roaring ahead. The fortnightly pattern was copied by IPC when they launched *Mizz* in November 1984.

Cover price is an arbitrary choice. The £1 coin has certainly established a price bridge-head and all the quality monthlies have reached at least that escarpment. The heavy glossies have reached £2 and have not suffered circulation set-backs on that score. There are myriad prices in between with most increases going for 10p when a couple of years before they would have been nervous in settling above 5p, even if they had repeated the dose in the same year. Most magazines judiciously watch their competitors in assessing the possible rate of increase. The dream of receiving enough net cover price (after trade discounts and distribution overheads) will always be thwarted with the fears of throttling the circulation, hence shedding advertising and therefore profit.

Of course, the magazine publisher has another choice, another route to take. He can join the ever-increasing clan of giving away the magazine to the reader absolutely free. He will still have distribution costs but no cover revenue. The disadvantage is obvious, but the advantage is that he can, up to a point, select his audience and establish his own circulation level. He can give away 5,000 copies or five million and then tell the advertisers of his circulation success. It is not a new phenomenon. The first recorded title was called *Modern Living with Gas* which was posted to all customers of North Thames Gas in 1938. The figures are ever changing but there certainly seem to be about 200 free magazines on the market with total circulation in excess of 26 million. You will be given a free magazine on every airline you fly with, or on Intercity trains, or by several shops or retail chains, or outside a tube station, or in a geographical area, or at the solicitors when you buy a house or at the estate agents in case you buy one. Your bank or credit company may send you a magazine, every hotel room seems to have one and your letter-box can be the recipient of all shapes and sizes of publications. The ACORN classification system of assessing neighbourhoods and class profiles has been a boundless incentive to some of the give-aways, whereas some of the earliest ones simply identified their potential reader in the street and proffered them a copy. (Some people achieve magazines and others have them thrust upon them.) *Girl about Town* has been published since 1972 and gives away about 125,000 copies a week. Their pre-selection seems to have deteriorated since the early days as the male half of the authors of this book is constantly having to refuse a copy at Oxford Circus tube station which is pushed towards him. It could be his walk.

Another factor to take into account when deciding which sort of magazine may attract a substantial and relevant portion of women readers is to bear in mind the solid mass of women served up by the Sunday colour magazines. There are six colour supplements and together they sell 11.5 million copies – or at least their mother newspapers do. The gross women's readership is some 15 million and the quality ones have become increasingly attractive to advertisers of fragrances, fashion and up-market household goods. The media group is popular with the media planners of the agencies because of the convenient numerical groupings and the not over-particular adherence to the rate cards, ensuring some attractive buys on the media schedule. To counterbalance the cost factor has to be weighed the editorial ambience which can frequently be at loggerheads with the advertisements. Liverpool heroin addicts, photographed in grainy verité, can clash with the facing page's advertisement for an elegant perfume, or the excitements of the African poaching scene, with disembowelled elephants in full colour, sit uneasily opposite an expensive winter coat. But the sheer numerical attraction, coupled with the art director's pleasure for a double-page spread to be seen in the very overt showcase at a Sunday breakfast, makes a formidable media choice. Women's magazine launchers cannot charge the cannons head-on and it is more important to consider the two important aspects of the launch: added value and branding. These are discussed later.

While searching for the Valhalla of that elusive (and illusionary) gap in the market, a glance at a breakdown of classifications in the women's press is salutary. Definitions get rather blurred but a reasonable attempt is as follows:

Teenage/pop	35
Home interest	25
Health/fitness	12
Hair and Beauty	10
Slimming	5
Fashion	15
General/life-style	27
Story	12
Babyhood/parents	9
Food	8

The divisions of the divisions are, of course, considerable, but any new attempt at scaling the market is going to fit into one or other of these compartments. Maybe we have cheated by going big for general and life-style but most of those titles do not fit into the sectionalised interests.

So is the market simply saturated with magazines? Are the bookshelves swamped with produce, not wanting and not being able to take any more? Have the big magazine houses carved up the market neatly between them to become reluctant to favour start-ups because of the internecine competition between their own existing titles? The answer to these questions is no, no and no. And the catalystic reason is competition. The bookstalls may seem to be awash with titles but there will also be an ebb and flow which will reflect changing tastes, styles and public appetites. The newstrade and the advertiser require, even if sometimes they think to the contrary, the energy and electricity of new titles. Titles will also slide away from the market as newer and better products take their place. This avoids the static or stagnant market and the hot breath of hard-edged competition is meat and drink to the magazine business which lives and dies out there in the cold compared to the feather-bedded hot-house enjoyed by the monopolistic world of commercial television.

Unfortunately there is no magic elixir of success to pass on to the potential launcher. In our original book we endeavoured to set out seven basic principles, or tenets, which might act as signposts. These were:

1. The initial concept
2. The editorial
3. Marketing
4. Launch impact
5. Publicity
6. Selling the product
7. Value for money

We see no reason to alter these but we would now add three more to help to meet today's conditions which make launching even more enigmatic than in 1978. These are:

8. Branding
9. Added value
10. Research

The initial concept is still, of course, the starting point, the kernel of the whole operation. It means that the magazine will be endowed with a single, initial idea, a concept which will help to isolate it clearly from all the other titles and quite plainly address itself to a specific market segment. We can illustrate this by looking at the titles which we have identified as launch successes: *Cosmopolitan, Company, Slimming, Home & Freezer Digest, Options, Just Seventeen, Elle, Country Living, Country Homes,*

Prima and *Best*, all well-defined ideas which were very positive in marking them out as different and positive.

It would be neat and tidy if we could say that all our Bad launches were devoid of a single good idea. Our list certainly contains some sloppy ideas: *Prima* (the first, not the German invasion) *Good Life, Candida, Eve, Personal, Inhabit, Rio, Kim, Etcetra, In Store*. But it also featured some failed titles which were perfectly sound basic notions like *Working Woman* and *Cachet*. Failures might be due to a loss of impact, an imperfect launch, a lack of on-going finance, a change of editor, a lack of nerve or simply a failure to come up with the editorial standards demanded by the initial concept.

The editorial will be discussed in a later chapter. It might be facile to say that great editors make great magazines, but there can be no doubt that indifferent editors can easily contribute to making indifferent magazines. Certainly all the success stories quoted have enjoyed the benefit of superbly professional editors and the contemporary standard of editors and art directors has probably never been higher. It cannot be otherwise in these days of such voracious competition. It is the art of publishing management today to fit the right editor into the right chair.

Marketing is a very elastic term these days but we use it here as the very practical manifestation of the exploitation of the excellent concept which has been hatched by the publishing company. It has to be positioned on the market in exactly the right way. The frequency of the magazine, the production values, the definition of the sought-after readership – these are the nuts and bolts of the launch. In our first book we took the liberty of quoting from a conference speech, *c.* 1978, made by Michael Bird, then of National Magazines and latterly of International Thomson. We felt that he made some interesting reflections on some of the basic options faced by the marketing manager and we do not apologise for repeating the comments here:

> In general I believe it is highly risky to launch a publication at people who currently do not buy magazines at all or who do not buy any of a particular category of magazines in the hope that these virgins, metaphorically speaking, will suddenly realise this is the publication they have been waiting for. The people who buy new magazines are mostly heavy readers of existing magazines. Although I am at present referring to medium to large circulation women's magazines, I suspect the same would apply to

specialised crafts and hobby magazines, girly mags, motoring magazines, etc. A 'gap in the market' should be treated as quicksand, at least until careful investigation proves otherwise. In short, one looks not for the low-pressure areas, but for high-pressure areas that still show signs of unfulfilled potential.

When pressed on the spur of the moment for a title for the conference paper, I came up with 'Innovation in Women's Magazines – the Fourth Dimension', partly in the hope that someone would ask me what such an outer space title could possibly mean. No one did. However, for the record, I will say that, as all fans of H.G. Wells and Dr Who will know, the fourth dimension is TIME. When magazine publishers talk of gaps or opportunities in markets, they often describe their markets in terms of age, class and sex or in terms of psychological or personality dimensions – but time is a crucial dimension – and an opportunity – often overlooked:

The freedom years – time that a woman can call her own: time that women did not possess and enjoy ten years ago.

The time-interval between issues of a successful monthly magazine. *Cosmopolitan* sells 90 per cent of its copies in two weeks. Both for the reader and the newsagent, the remaining two weeks are a gap to be filled.

Lastly, it is vital to choose the right time, socially and economically, to bring out a new publication. Are the readers ready? Is the advertising available?

Some lessons:

- Exploit 'high-pressure' areas in the market, not too low-pressure areas.
- The biggest gap in the market is the time-interval between October and November issues of a successful magazine.
- Discard the 'zero-sum' mentality: the size of a market is elastic, up *and* down.
- Timing is critical: too early is as bad as too late.
- Aim at a clearly-defined audience.
- Learn from other countries, but don't imitate.
- A simple idea professionally executed is better than a brilliant idea which is handled amateurishly or half-heartedly.

The launch impact speaks for itself. Whether the launch is to receive the full treatment, with the massive dose of multi-media advertising, or is to have to almost sneak out on to the market backed only with a good idea and a lot of faith, or even to be brought in front of the public as a test or pilot, the maximum impact has to be made. This is the moment of truth – if the launch moment is foozled or half-hearted, it can never be relived. A new magazine is like a West End show. Everyone wants to know what it is like and how good, or bad, it is. The glamour of the opening night with the searchlight of attention is the moment when the show is made or broken. Get it right and you are giving your tyro magazine the best possible chance in life – get it wrong and that can be the beginning of the end. That impact has to be made, of course, not only on the potential reader but also on the advertiser and the newstrade. Whether your publicity is in pounds and pence, or relying on PR and word of mouth, this is your moment.

The product has to be sold to many people at the same time and PR can play an immense role. The daily press and the electronic media can be manipulated with a great deal of hard work and ingenuity. A new magazine is news. A *successful* new magazine is big news. The newstrade and the advertiser will want to be told and kept informed of the progress of the launch – by personal presentation, trade press advertising and, again, effective PR.

Value for money is the new necessity as cover prices have steadily risen. The fact that paper has been a soaring commodity, even if print prices have generally remained behind inflation (as well as editorial and advertisement salaries, as more magazines have been in competition for better staff), means little or nothing to the magazine buyer. She looks for value, particularly when her house probably gets two or three Sunday colour supplements, ostensibly full of colour pages, plopping through her letter box absolutely free. To her, magazines have been costing more and more each year and for her £1, £1.25 or £2 she expects lots of editorial pages and lots of colour. She likes the tactile experience of good paper so that when she has bought her magazine she gets a treat. She will not be short-changed on value and she does actually recognise the difference between advertising pages and editorial pages. She will complain to the editor or the publisher when the big autumn issues seem to represent bad value, i.e. too many advertising pages. She is probably the same reader who complains when January issues are thin and, therefore, she gets bad value. The fact may well be, of course, that she will actually get more editorial pages in January than November because the issue has to be bulked up.

Most magazines have a basic book so that the editorial quantity never sinks below a prescribed formula and editorial pages are added in proportion to extra advertising pages. The home magazines and the fashion magazines tend to score here because their readers are probably looking for a new kitchen or a new winter coat and the many advertising pages simply extend the available choice and selection. But thicker magazines are perceived as better value for money. The 'doorstep' appearance of one or two of the glossies, when the paging reaches as much as 500, may be contrary to this maxim as they can perhaps be a little forbidding to the busy reader.

'Branding' is the newer word in the publishers' vocabulary. Consumer goods have been branded for years but of late publishers have tended to realise that their magazine has to be isolated from the competition. They must represent a positive market segment and sit in a positive site in that market segment. *Prima* recognised this. A magazine like *Good Housekeeping*, backed with the great resources of the Good Housekeeping Institute and a continuous book publishing programme, is a perfect example. The two new country magazines have positioned themselves, each rather differently, in the market. *Just Seventeen* is branded very clearly in its own segment, just as *Vogue* has been since 1916. At two extremes of the intelligence quotient sit *Harpers & Queen* and *Chat* – both branded clearly. The magazines which will fail in their attempts to clamber onto the bookstalls will be the ones which have not clearly distinguished themselves from the rest of the competition so that the reader, and certainly the advertiser, does not acknowledge or recognise what the magazine is trying to do or to whom it is trying to speak. It must, in the current American publishing vernacular 'have a mission'.

'Added value' is another perceived necessity. Once the magazine is seen as having a brand positioning it is necessary to give it some added value which will prompt reader purchase and advertiser interest. Again we quote *Prima* as having acknowledged this need. Every issue contains a paper pattern which is certainly recognised by the reader as being added to the value of the magazine. The IPC not so look unalike called *Essentials* also carried a paper pattern but, to add icing to the cake, also gave away ring binders with the first issue and provided a perforated section to be removed and filed away in the ring binder – a sort of magazine Filofax. The Emap magazine *More!* has a 12-page pull-out on shop merchandise. These are very overt examples but new magazines will certainly be asking their marketing departments for bright ideas. The advertisers will also be provided with value-added ideas which will give one magazine an advantage over its competitors – more than cost per thousand advantages, or sheer circulation or readership statistics, but a very positive plus which will present the case for the magazine in a better light. This is a defensive move as the media shops and the agency media departments try to convert the media into a commodity, to be bought like cocoa or tin. If the advertiser (that is the company which actually pays the money) is convinced of the particular plus factor that will make a magazine important to him he will override the media buyers (who was it who called them 'seventeen-year-old horsethieves with calculators?) and want his advertising placed in that magazine. It may be an editorial value or a marketing value but either way magazines, and in particular new titles, will be searching for their added value factor.

Our final maxim is research. This, of course, is totally out of chronological order because after the initial concept the magazine idea has to be researched. The days of the sudden idea being swiftly converted to a paper and print reality are virtually over. The massive cost and risk of launches are just too high for the publisher to enjoy an adventure playground. The idea, with or without a dummy, has to be researched to test the love, hate, or utter indifference of the potential audience. Sometimes this research will take the form of group discussions when a number of carefully weighted readers will be gathered together to discuss the project, even if they are not to be told what the idea actually is. Sometimes the research will be by interview – a straight opinion poll. It would be a foolhardy launcher who does not research because the 'seat of the pants' days are gone. Research is only a tool and can only be a guide to how a market is thinking and what they are feeling. Sometimes research can get it wrong (*Cosmopolitan* was told in 1971 that the magazine would not succeed in this country as British women were not overly interested in sex). But with the right questions the research factor, coupled with all the other processes and agonies which the publisher has to weigh up, is a vital element in the do-we-jump decision. Research will also be employed in assessing the opinions of the advertiser and the newstrade. The marketing department of the publisher will also be carrying out their own research to assess the size and trends of the market, the demographics and income patterns of the readership, the advertising expenditure patterns and priorities, the state of the competition in circulation, readership, advertisement value and revenue and an examination of the possibilities of other entrants into the market.

So there we have it. To launch or not to launch, what, when or why. You have your great idea and research has demonstrated to you that the reader is out there, the newstrade is enthusiastic and the advertiser is interested in investing his advertising pounds with you. You then only have to worry about your editorial concept and objectives, your positioning statements, your branding, your added value ingredient, the appointment of your editor and the staff, your choice of advertisement director and sales team, your circulation and distribution arrangements, your rate card structure, your production specifications, your printing methods, your promotion budgets, your accommodation and office requirements, your business plan, your financing, your market considerations, your commercial structure, your contingency plans, your launch strategy, your presentation programme and technique, your appointment of an advertising agency, your selection of a public relations company, your publicity budgets, your launch parties and the date of launch.

And your launch may actually succeed.

8

SELLING AND BUYING OF SPACE

While over the last ten years there has been a decline in women's general, down-market and weekly titles, there has been a growing number of monthlies appearing in the specialised titles, catering for specific interest and life-style, ie beauty/fashion, health and fitness, country, food/homes etc.

As a sales operation to the advertising industry, women's magazines represent an important market force. There are 69 monthly, weekly and bi-monthly titles on the NRS (July 1986–June 1987).

Alone, women's weeklies reach an estimated 9.8 million women in an average week and a further two million men. Add to this the coverage of the 40 women's monthlies of 10.4 million women and another 3.6 million men, not including the readership or circulation of the other 76 women's titles which do not appear on the NRS, and a fantastic marketplace emerges.

The industry delivers every type of female – teenagers, working independent girls, home-buyers, young mothers, families, mature women and grandmothers, each one with different age/class profiles, causing a hive of activity amongst the 12 or so magazine publishing houses (bearing in mind that 75 per cent of revenue has to come from the advertising revenue), not forgetting the competition from other media – newspapers, regional press, TV, radio, posters, cinema, direct mail – all fighting for their share of the advertising cake.

The business of selling advertising space has, over the past ten years, become very sophisticated, with each and every magazine selling in its own particular way, conducive to its problems. Of course, good salespeople will always have their own individual personalities

117

and this, together with enthusiasm, coupled with knowledge of their magazine, can be a great advantage. Being a salesperson gives one a chance of human contact, different attitudes of debate, a psychological understanding of various types of audience and a platform to express oneself authoritatively and persuasively.

The media salesperson's job is becoming more demanding and more complex each year. Continuous rises in production costs and the effort in maintaining sales, while improving the product all the time, grows and, therefore, the skills of the salespeople become more and more important to the economy of the publication for which they work.

The continuing relationship between the buyer and seller of space will always be delicate and even bellicose. The buyers and planners in the agencies and the media shops are spoilt for choice with the plethora of media at their disposal. There is much time-wasting and poor presentation by some of the salespeople and brusqueness and lack of courtesy by the receiving end. But this is all part of the game of buying and selling and the successful salesperson will make the right sort of call, at the right level, at the right time. This is a communication business and it is vital that both sides are aware of the other's problems and strategies. The good salesperson will have been briefed on the market position and timing of the campaign before going to the agency. The buyer will be interested to learn of new developments in the magazine, such as editorial changes, in order to be up to date. Of course, not all selling is to the agency. The client will often come into the picture. It *is* his money which is being spent and many clients are keenly aware of the media market available to them. Magazines can score heavily here because their medium is more personal than the anonymous world of television or the national newspapers. The client, in a particular field, will probably already know, or want to know, the editor or the appropriate departmental editor of the magazines which he advertises in, or might advertise in. This gives the magazine the opportunity of in-house presentations, attended by the suitable editorial staff, to give the client the atmosphere and ambience of the magazine.

Again the client will be very aware of the changes in his market place which can be effected by the magazines. He has only *one* interest in life – the success of his product. The agency buyer will have a dozen accounts in various fields.

Research Studies

The contemporary salesperson has the advantage of extensive research to back the magazine's sales case. Marketing departments can now provide research and information to help in marketing to both advertisers and consumers, with the National Readership Survey and the Target Group Index.

NRS is administered by JICNARS and the method is personal interviews on a random sample of 28,000 throughout the year on frequency and recency of reading. This covers over 200 newspapers and magazines – on demographics, life-style data and other media.

TGI is produced by BMRB. It is self-administered by leaving a questionnaire with a random sample of 24,000 throughout the year, weighted to NRS, and covers some 130 newspapers and magazines, product and brand usage.

There has been an addition of 'Life-style' statements to the 1984 survey. BMRB asked TGI respondents to indicate their agreement or disagreement with a range of statements about their attitudes and opinions on a variety of topics. This has added another, more qualitative, dimension to existing research on product usage and media consumption, by linking people's behaviour to their stated opinions.

Using multivariate computer analysis techniques, such as cluster analysis, it has been possible to use the TGI 'Life-style' data to discover discrete groups with distinct 'personalities'.

The Media Involvement Study

Published by the Magazine Marketplace Group in 1984, was an original piece of research funded by a group of ten magazine publishers. The survey was designed to discover the way people use and regard different media, which in turn determines their chances of seeing any advertisements carried and also influences their reaction to them. Magazines were rated as the best source of ideas and information for 15 out of the 22 interest areas covered by the research.

Multiplying the Media Effect

Published by the Magazine Marketplace Group, following original research in 1985. They sponsored a research programme designed to investigate the way in which television and magazine advertisements communicate with their audience, and, in particular, the interaction between the two media. The findings are of value to those making media policy decisions, and to creative people devising mixed media campaigns. The results demonstrated that television and magazines working together in a campaign produce a fuller, richer and more effective communication than either medium can achieve alone.

The MPX Readership Study

Research into magazine page exposure carried out in 1986, sponsored by six magazine publishers. It covered 110 magazines plus the Sunday supplements, and was designed to estimate reader exposure to the magazine advertising over and above the average issue readership estimated by the National Readership Survey. The research shows the average magazine page is read or looked at 1.8 times by the reader.

Neighbourhood Classifications

Developed to categorise consumers (and readers) according to the type of residential area in which they live. ACORN, MOSAIC, PINPOINT, SUPERPROFILE are examples of cluster analyses which use census variables and other nationally available data to identify neighbourhood types, based on the observation that people in similar housing types and in close proximity tend to share similar demographic and consumer characteristics. Analysis of NRS and TGI respondents' postcodes allows analysis of magazine readers by their propensity to dwell in particular types of neighbourhood.

Lifestage Classifications

Developed to classify consumers (and readers) according to their stage in family development. SAGACITY is an example of a lifestage classification which uses data collected on the NRS to identify groups of the population at different stages of family formation, with subdivisions into white collar/blue collar and better off/worse off.

Media Monitoring Services

Information of the advertising content of different media. Recent years have seen the development of a range of competing services which monitor the advertising content, in volume or value, of television, radio, newspapers and magazines.

Examples of such services are:

- MEAL (Media Expenditure Analysis Limited)
- Magazine Monitor/Brand Monitor
- IMS Medialog
- The Media Register
- The Auditor
- Media Audits

It is pleasing to note that agencies are becoming more open minded about first reader/purchaser research and more willing to accept it. It gives a much stronger impression of who actually spends money to read the magazine. One should not forget that the reasons why agencies and clients use women's magazines is not only due to the importance of women in terms of purchasing power, but because of the opportunity that magazines offer advertisers of speaking directly to women. As already stated, magazines can offer effective coverage of women – 42 per cent coverage of all women through the women's weekly field and 45 per cent via the women's monthly market can be achieved. Of course, to buy this type of coverage would require a great deal of money and would make for a great deal of wastage – market segmentation thus plays a very important role.

The advantages of selling via women's magazines is precise targeting and selectivity, complimentary environment, back reference, reaching light TV viewers, coupon response, image building and the chance for multiple exposure.

One should remember that the best selling aid is often the editor. She is the very heartbeat of the magazine – she is the one to relay the real sales message and 30 minutes listening to her is of great value, both to the salesperson and buyer alike. You cannot feed 'atmosphere' into a computer. We very much believe in getting editors involved with advertisers and agencies. We still believe in individual selling and not groups. Each and every magazine has its own personality.

This policy is by no means general in the magazine business; one large conglomerate believes in the group sell across the board, with one salesman selling across a range of titles. We cannot agree and think this is bad for buyer and seller alike. The life of the weakest titles in the group is also artificially prolonged by really cheap 'buys' on the group deal. Alternatively, the weakest title may die by neglect as it is more attractive for the salesman to concentrate on the blue chip titles. If the weaker title has its own staff, solely devoted to it, then their enthusiasm and loyalty will generate life into it – provided, of course, that this is not a lost cause. We feel that if the magazine has any chance of survival this is more likely to be achieved by the careful nursing of the individual staff than by treating it as the twenty-eighth title on the list, added as makeweight to a computerised deal.

It is argued that the group sale also makes for an advantageous discount buy but we feel that group or indeed single discounts are an inherent sign of weakness. The rates for the magazine should have been assessed on the magazine's value in the market, its circulation and readership and, of course, its cost to produce. The rate card produced out of these factors should be 'hard', given the customary modicum of bargaining on the edge of that hard card. However, there is a 'bully-boy' technique operated by a certain breed of buyer, which goes for the kill in every piece of alleged buying, often happy to purchase quantity rather than quality. Happily, an increasing number of buyers now take environment instead of sheer numbers into consideration and judge each magazine accordingly.

We believe in the individualistic sell – with the truly efficient salesman standing out and being remembered for his unique sales technique. It must surely be refreshing for a client to be approached by a salesman who says, 'Here is my magazine – this is where your product can create sales, and this is how to do it.' Such a strong creative approach must sound better than the so-often heard, 'I see you're using such and such a magazine – why not use ours?' It is enthusiasm, creative selling and total involvement which makes the sales proposition more interesting for the client (and the salesman) and is certainly more likely to produce a sale. Much time and effort is expended in researching information and pinpointing any problems the client may have in distribution or moving into a new market. Even a rough idea for an advertising campaign, however ingenuous it may be, displays enthusiasm and interest. Clients can be flattered and impressed that the magazine seems to care, creating a rapport which is worth a great deal in the buying/selling relationship.

A natural target for the magazine salesman is the advertising in other titles, but the true market is any advertising relevant to the audience offered by a particular magazine. There is no reason why any newspaper or television advertiser should not also become a magazine advertiser, perhaps as part of a media mix. The good salesman will not be inhibited by the use of other media to the exclusion of his own and will realise that his competitor is just as likely to be a particular local radio station as another women's magazine. Young women's magazines in particular, with readerships which are not as TV-saturated as the older generations, have a particularly strong case for a share of some of the television advertising. But the conquest of these fields calls for an increasing use of the creative sales pitch – these pitches have to be well researched and prepared and must present feasible prospects.

An advertising presentation to a group of clients, or to an agency, can be very effective, but not if it's going to be a magic lantern show with rather a dreary parade of NRS and TGI material. The presentation should show the heart of the magazine, with some emphasis on the editorial ethos, and should demonstrate the life-style of the magazine and its readers as well as a commercial assessment. Know your audience, know your subject and keep it simple. Needless to say, it should be technically perfect, well rehearsed and timed! If this seems an unnecessary statement, it is because we have seen some appalling presentations, some of which have started (after the audience had assembled), with a request for the whereabouts of an electric socket!

Another, and very specialised part of the sales technique, is the launch of a new title. For the publisher this is one of the most exciting parts of the whole business as he creates the concept and gets involved with the co-ordination of the editorial and business functions. However, the salesman concerned with the launch needs different skills from those involved in the on-going sales of an established publication. He has a dummy and a concept and perhaps some basic research of the proposed target audience. He is backed by the editorial aims of the new title and probably the strength of a publicity expenditure in the trade press to give the launch excitement. Against this background the skill and efforts of the salesman are put to the fullest use. Here is real creative selling where the 'anything for me today?' ploy is utterly useless. It is quite a battlefield out there, armed with your new rate card and your dummy publication, but it can be the making of the good salesman. Needless to say the achievements of the sales staff on the launch are vital to the economy of the new title, and the character of the advertising they sell will help to mould the character of the magazine itself. By this we mean resisting the temptation inherent in the easy sell of the categories of advertising that a more established title would eschew – the wholesale booking of such space will denigrate the class of the new magazine. Too often we have seen this temptation yielded to – with the subsequent 'turn off' by the quality advertisers which the magazine wanted to attract in the first place.

Time is not on the side of the launch salesman. He probably has six months from the 'off' to the first published issue, and his campaign of action has to be planned in detail – there is no time for random calls. He has the difficult task of communicating his new magazine's qualitative aspects and atmosphere ahead of its birth to the advertising world. His category priorities must be right and he will have to sell as hard to the client as the agency. Certain agencies are notorious for their disinterest in new magazines until they have proved themselves, preferably waiting for the first ABC figures and the appearance on the NRS. Fortunately, this attitude is receding and more of the younger media directors and independents are prepared to step in where angels fear to tread. This is a fortunate trend as advertisers have a certain ovine quality in their make-up and will follow the flock. Our experience on many launches has shown that the larger agencies tend to be less experimental and the smaller ones are likely to be more entrepreneurial in their attitudes. Because of the shortage of time the launch sales staff have to use more commando tactics than usual, with an aggressive technique. The virtues of honesty and hard work, backed with all the facts available, will triumph. Anything less, we promise you, will fail in the end!

Without wishing to be accused of overgeneralisation, we are aware that some of the big agencies have become sectionalised to the extent of sometimes losing sight of the ultimate objective. The media department can become out of touch not only with the client but with their own account group. The fierce competition of the buying world dominates the media buyer's life to the extent of a search for the cheapest quantity at the expense of the identifiable quality. Smaller agencies often impress us more – the media director of the smaller unit being in direct and constant touch with his client and thus acquiring a deeper and more incisive knowledge of the client's business and that of his competitors.

On the broader aspect of selling and buying is the perennial question of positioning. Apart from the day-to-day arguments of the rate for the space, there is the demand for the specific positioning of the advertising purchased. As buying has tended to become more sophisticated, and the women's magazines have grown fatter with more competitive advertising, more and more special premium positions have been created and demanded. These may vary from the simple, and almost mandatory, demand for 'right-hand page, front of book' to the positive and explicit purchase of a page facing a particular and popular editorial feature. Magazines, bombarded by such buying, have brought in premium prices and will charge extra percentages on the first half of the magazine as well as the customary premiums like facing matter and bleed. There has also been a complicated inclination to earmark the actual spreads in the magazine with an agency negotiating for, say, the fifth colour spread in the book. We say 'complicated' because of the subsequent inflexibility available to the magazine and the problems it brings to both the editor and advertisement department. There is obviously a saturation point which can be quickly reached early in the year by a number of big advertisers, limiting the advertisement director's manoeuvrability in selling his space or satisfactorily building up the make-up of a well-balanced book.

While a certain amount of premium buying is the name of the game it can reach unacceptable levels for both sides. It can also be fallacious when the myths that grow up around magazine space buying become creeds.

If the buyer does his homework on the magazine he wishes to place his business with, he should then buy creatively, positioning next to/ near relevant editorial, not insisting on being first or second spread or right hand in the book. A rather bad example of this was an advertiser promoting his quality beef amongst high-fashion advertisers. It stood out like a sore thumb and we feel sure that the other advertisers were not happy. The magazine in question has a superb cookery feature every month, where the beef advertisement would have sat happily and gained more 'goodwill' and coverage next to relevant editorial.

The size of the issue, the front or back half, right- or left-hand pages, really does not matter. The crucial factor is the power of the creative appeal of a particular advertisement, rather than its placing in the magazine. Of course, it goes without saying that the power of a double page spread must be greater than a single page etc, but one would get greater value out of more considerate placing of advertisements in the right magazine in the right environmental position.

We believe that advertisers should be more adventurous with their space sizes and editors more willing to accept them. We should all be more futuristic and try new approaches. A certain creative magazine, for instance, will not accept unusual shapes and sizes of advertisement – how can its publishers, therefore, call it creative?

Below-the-line promotions are becoming more the norm. Often this cuts out the agencies with the publisher producing the copy for the advertiser. This type of advertising assists the advertisement department to obtain extra multiple pages of space by devising 'advertorials', either solely for an advertiser or partnership advertising pages, such as shoes and stockings, cars and clothes etc, plus whole seasonal campaigns. In return, the advertiser gets an editorial-type advertisement with the opportunity of merchandising to back this up, ie brochures and mailings to store buyers and merchandising managers, window and in-store displays.

Magazine publishers, like all other media owners, are under constant threat of rate discounting. It is, of course, the buyer's job to get space at the cheapest possible rate where the publisher has to sell it at the highest rate to give him the best yield per page. The average net revenue is very important. The magazine product is certainly not perishable – the paging can be adjusted as desired, the only factor being economic. The cost of producing a single sheet of paper by the photogravure process is expensive and is carefully calculated. It does not always prove to be the right equation simply to add more pages to a certain size issue – the magazine can actually lose money by adding pages. There are buyers of advertising who find this hard to believe – to them any money they care to lavish on the magazines must be more than welcome. But if the economics of the magazine have been calculated correctly then the cost of advertising as offered on the rate card is the right rate for the job – all factors taken into account.

This should apply to all magazines and means that when a big advertiser demands discounts or a sharp buying unit of an agency wants a substantial cut on the rate card, it will eventually lead to an inevitable conclusion: the advertisement rates will have to be increased. Since this action will lead to the same advertisers and agencies demanding more discounts, the publisher will be in danger of moving his magazine into a rate area which is too expensive for what he has to offer. Then the hard-nosed buyer will leave him anyway – and the magazine will be free to slide gently out of business! This may seem an exaggeration but the simple truth remains: one man's discount is another man's rate increase.

There is another peril facing the magazine business, which is the collective buy. A group of companies will give one agency media department, or a media shop, the lucrative task of buying all the space for all the companies in the group. This can be a bonanza for the buyer as he immediately commences to bulk-buy his space from the magazines. He is suddenly handed such power that he can even group deal with several titles in the same magazine house. If you don't want to play, his intention will be for you to kiss goodbye to half a dozen accounts, all of whom may have been buying space in your magazine before. Such catastrophes can, will and do happen – to the detriment of the magazine and damaging, ultimately, to the interests of the client. Chunks of space bought at discount could destroy magazines if the practice is not resisted. Centralised media buying is a backward step for the magazine industry which should be getting the proper rate for the job in order to invest in the editorial and production quality of the magazines, rather than to clamber on to the slippery slopes of flash discounting.

The opportunities for magazine selling are immense as television viewing is demonstrably declining and becoming increasingly expensive. The magazine medium is proliferating and circulations increasing for the successful titles. We discuss rate discounting in our last chapter but we must emphasise here that magazines will be doomed to eventual destruction if they allow themselves to be treated as a buying commodity and lose the opportunity of selling and presenting their individual merits to the buyers. The cry is 'Sell-and Survive'.

9

CIRCULATION AND DISTRIBUTION

This is not the most opportune time to be writing about the circulation of magazines because the distribution industry has never been in such a state of flux or turmoil. It has always been a complicated, almost esoteric, network of retailers, wholesalers and distributors but endeavours have been made in recent years to rationalise the expensive and labyrinthine process of getting a magazine from printer to reader, and those endeavours are chiefly due to the newer intake of executives coming into the industry.

The whole machinery is becoming modernised as marketing methods, often long employed in other businesses, are coming more and more to the fore. Indeed, words like marketing, merchandising, precision targeting and computing are bandied about as the normal lingua franca of the industry – words which would have been met with puzzled frowns by the wholesalers and retailers of yesteryear. The reason why there has been such an explosion of expertise is simple: the massive increase in the amount of product endeavouring to find its way not only into the shops *per se*, but into the right sort of shop in the right sort of location with the right sort of potential customer.

Up until recently there was a willy-nilly approach to the whole operation. A network of wholesalers, large and small, were stretched across the UK. The principal wholesalers were W H Smith, John Menzies (the Scottish company who had mopped up Wymans) and Surridge Dawson. The first two are also, of course, extensive retailers but not necessarily customers of the parent company's wholesalers. A wholesaler could have retailer customers all over his territory and common-sense began to prevail a couple of years ago when the rationalisation of the provinces became the norm – in short, a division of the retail customers into geographically convenient locations. London saw a similar rationalisation in August 1987 with not a little heated discussion and occasional cries of pain. To add fuel to the fire, Rupert Murdoch announced in November 1987 that he would re-draw the map of the wholesale trade by appointing only 182 areas of wholesale in England and Wales to handle his newspapers (and magazines in time). This sent a scream through the trade although many of the big groups, confident of being appointed, were whistling in the dark. Where Murdoch treads Maxwell is never far behind and the Periodical Proprietors Association (PPA) started to make noises that they too would come up with their own package. Magazines, of course, require a different kind of distribution service from newspapers but the fact that periodical and magazine publishers claim an annual distribution worth of £500 million to the trade concentrates the mind. Whatever happens, a major shake-up of old-established systems will feature strongly in the late 1980s.

There is little likelihood that the real power will not continue to remain with the leading trinity of W H Smith, with 35 per cent, John Menzies with 25 per cent, and Surridge Dawson with 10 per cent. They have become increasingly efficient over the years and have all introduced computerised systems to ensure that the most suitable titles get into the most suitable locations. In crude terms, a copy of *Harpers & Queen* is more likely to sell in Mayfair than Bootle and a copy of *Chat* will be more favourably received in Gateshead than Belgravia. Having stated the obvious, the ACORN survey (A Classification of Residential Neighbourhoods) will be able to help to distinguish the most apt areas within the connurbations.

The retailer (the CTN) is the front line of the whole complicated magazine war. The retailer takes 25 per cent of the cover price. (The wholesaler takes 15 per cent and the publisher 60 per cent.) Retailers tend to be like farmers – the weather is never exactly right. There are always divergent views about the exact numbers of retail outlets and how many have disappeared or are about to disappear. The Euromonitor Report, published in 1986, forecast that 3,300 shops would disappear in five years. One in seven shops in the UK is a CTN with 48,000 shops operating in 1984. But people are smoking less, and eating fewer sweets, and tobacco products account for 36 per cent of a typical CTN's sales. Tobacco sales have fallen by some 35 per cent in a decade which is bad news for the CTN but, of course, may concentrate their minds more on the news side of the business. The majority of the retail outlets are independent (corner shop, family business etc) and there are big CTN multiples like W H Smith, John Menzies, Martin Retail Group, Forbuoys plc, Preedy and Finlays. In addition there are convenience stores, selling milk and groceries and magazines from early till late. There were about 700 in 1986 and the forecast number by 1990 was about 4,200.

We also have to mention supermarkets because they will inevitably and substantially enter the news fray in the next decade. There are about 6,000 supermarkets in the UK and only some 5 per cent (the figure grows steadily) stock magazines. ASDA have sold 'news' for about ten years and Tesco are now taking magazines very seriously. At the time of writing even Sainsbury are making cautious experiments. The sale of women's magazines in supermarkets is as natural as night following day but progress is slow, not least on the side of the publishers and the distributors who are circumspect about upsetting the traditional news agent trade. But as long as the supplies are handled by the local wholesaler, and the resultant sales are not seen to disrupt sales in the neighbouring CTNs, news will steadily advance into supermarkets. Of course, *Family Circle* and *Living*, the duo published by International Thomson, are still exclusively sited at the lucrative check-outs and the rest of the trade have to be satisfied with displays within, or sometimes outside, the check-out area. But tens of thousands of women shoppers tramp each week through the cavernous supermarkets and if they are stopping smoking or chocolate-munching they are not going to appear in the local CTN. It is a vast trade for the women's magazine publishers to capture, particularly the weeklies and the home interest monthlies. If it pays the supermarkets to carry magazine stock (and they get more profitable as cover prices rise) then they will not eschew the magazine trade. Publishers, naturally, expect that their sales will increase dramatically and positively, rather than simply shift from one sort of outlet to another. Of course, bar coding will have to appear on front covers.

The distributor is a power in the world of publishing. Up to comparatively recently most of the larger publishing houses employed their own in-house circulation departments with their own sales force around the country. Over the past 15 years a new sub-industry has evolved, frequently run as an adjunct of each publishing group to handle their own client titles but also to sell and distribute third-party sales. This means that a distributor will often handle competition titles. Comag, for instance, which was one of the first companies set up is wholly owned by the National Magazine Company and Condé Nast so that their sales force sells *Vogue, Harpers & Queen, The Tatler, Good Housekeeping, House & Garden, World of Interiors* and all the other titles from the two owner-publishing groups. But, additionally, they also distribute some 230 other titles, whether or not they are competitive. There are over 20 other distributors handling about 1,200 UK titles and 800 imported titles between them. To boggle the mind further, they act for about 470 publishers. Even IPC, who have long remained sniffily aloof, have now formed a distribution unit to handle third-party publishers. Many of the distributors also claim to be experts in marketing so that they are particularly helpful to publishers entering the battle with new launches. They can provide statistical and trade information, advise on budgets, print orders, launching techniques, frequency of publishing and all the other relevant material which a publisher so desperately requires before taking the plunge. Some of the larger distributors run retail audits, merchandising schemes and other checks on the progress of the client's publication, or his competitors', on the marketplace. The biggest and most successful distributors have constant approaches to take on new clients, or someone else's erstwhile one, and it is interesting to see the check-list published by Comag in one of the 1987 editions of their own trade magazine.

What are we looking for in assessing the success of a proposed magazine? Let us outline a few main points:

Who is the magazine aimed at?

Can they find the same information or entertainment elsewhere – not necessarily in a magazine?

Why should they buy your magazine rather than any other?

It may seem obvious but many would-be publishers forget to ask themselves these questions. A publication without a clearly defined target market is almost certainly doomed to failure.

How many people are there in your target market and what penetration into the market do you anticipate? For example, a publication aimed at teenage girls could identify a 1.7 million target audience between the ages of 13 and 15. A 5% penetration delivers a sale of 85,000 in this market.

Having put a figure on the size of your market and the penetration you hope to achieve, how many copies of the launch issue do you intend to distribute?

How many copies will you be distributing, and selling, by issue No 6? Are these figures realistic?

What is your break-even point in terms of copy sales? What is the strength of competition in your market? How will your publication compete on price, pagination, format, frequency, colour content, editorial/advertisement ratio?

What size of budget have you allocated for promotion? Many magazines fail because the target market is not aware of their existence. It is unrealistic to rely on P.R. to spread the word.

When do you intend to launch your publication? Why have you chosen this date?

Does your launch coincide with a Bank Holiday or the launch of another publication?

Is there a viable advertisement market in the market sector you have chosen?

How important are ad sales to the success of your venture?

How many staff will you need to produce your publication?

Have you secured adequate finance to ensure the survival of your publication until you start receiving payment from your advertisers and your news-stand distribution?

Have you produced a dummy issue or at least an artwork indication of the front cover?

These questions are fundamental in planning a successful magazine launch; it is all too easy to be carried away with enthusiasm without ensuring that the project is based on sound commercial principles.

As the years unfold and the whole business of getting magazine from printer to reader gets more complicated, more confusing and more expensive, the relationship between publisher, distributor, wholesaler and retailer will get more involved. Great sheets of green computer paper will continue to proliferate as well as all the machinery of the increasingly complex trade. The distributor will be market-led and will be the eyes and ears of the publisher: the future of the retail outlets, competitive activity, trade views and opinions, cover price advice, budgets, future potential, forward planning, print order forecasting, a feed-back on information, trade intelligence – rather than simple, and hopefully honest, brokerage.

We crave a little indulgence here to introduce a lighter, but we hope incisive note, on this essential factor in the publisher–distribution relationship. In an article in *The Publisher* in June 1983 one of the authors of this book outlined some of the problems.

But we have appointed a Distributor. We used to think that a Distributor was an essential part of the internal combustion engine. We try to convince ourselves that he is also an essential part of the lengthy and rather tardy part of the distribution process. Distributors come in all shapes and sizes, fat, lean, blue-eyed, dark-jowled, clean-limbed, shifty, grumpy and, sometimes, handsome. They are the essential link in the chain, they tell us, between Publisher and stockist. The Distributor is, in the words of the late W.C. Fields, the Abyssinian in the wood-supply. They rabbit on about publicity spending, s.o.r., wholesalers orders, marketing concept, brokerage and all sorts of other complications to the pure and simple life.

After a working lifetime of publishing magazines I now have some firm ideas about the Publisher/Distributor working relationship and at the invitation of the Editor of this new and long-overdue journal, I am happy to share them with my fellow Publishers:

1. *The Haywards Heath Syndrome*. So called because it is always at a place like Haywards Heath railway bookstall that your Editor lands up on a wet, winter Sunday. There is no copy of her magazine at the bookstall. Consternation! Or worse, there are dozens of copies of her magazine at the bookstall. More consternation! Why (*a*) can't the Publisher ensure adequate supplies and (*b*) why does the Publisher waste time and money pumping copies into the unwilling hands of the uneducated, ignorant clods of Haywards Heath?

Action: phone your Distributor who will whinge and immediately send urgent supplies to Hampstead Heath.

2. *Exclusivity*. Of course, you will be horrified to discover that your Distributor not only handles your title *Doggy World* but also your competitors: *Woof, Bark, Our Canines* and *New Dog*.

Action: fire the Distributor or start a magazine for Cats.

3. *Publicity*. You have dug deep, seen the bank manager and budgeted £25.00 for an across-the-board publicity campaign to include national press, television and network radio. Again, your miserable Distributor will be unsatisfied and demand double the money, telling you that the trade will not be impressed.

Action: try sandwich boards.

4. *Personal appearances*. You decide that you ought to get out and about and meet the chaps in the wholesale trade. You have an incredibly good and witty speech, no more than one and a half hours. Distributor tells you they

will need food and drink as well.

Is the man never happy?

Action: try sandwiches.

5. *Computeritis*. Your Distributor will blind you with science with his computer. He can tell you that you have just sold a copy of *Doggy World* to a little old lady in Worcester. The information is not too lapel-grabbing to you, particularly when the computer tells you that you haven't sold a copy of *Doggy World* to the other 8.6 million dog owners.

Action: it's OK because your bill is also on the computer and you won't get it till Christmas.

There is another method of distributing magazines which has been underemployed in this country, although widely used in the USA. This is subscription selling. The phrase has often had a pejorative echo about it in the UK but it has been operated with tremendous effect and success by *Reader's Digest* who maintain an incredible monthly circulation of about 1.6 million copies almost entirely by subscription. The arguments against subscriptions have been legion: too expensive, bad renewal rate, difficult to obtain, even more difficult to service and, anyhow, rather unBritish. All these objections can be, and recently have been, overcome and we think that women's magazines will find subscriptions can produce a very useful extra source of ABC circulation with subsidiary benefits.

The British woman has always been used to buying her magazine from the local news agent or the local multiple. It is certainly not difficult to buy a magazine in this country – at the railway station, at the corner shop, in the convenience store, perhaps in the supermarket or from the street kiosk. Her American cousin has been much more accustomed to magazines arriving by post, along with the Sears Roebuck catalogue and all the other mail order trappings which make American retailing go round and round. She is also possibly not so conveniently placed to buy her magazine if she lives on a farm in the Bible belt. Supermarkets and drug stores certainly sell magazines in the USA but the fact is that the big monthly titles have traditionally expected to sell about two-thirds of their huge circulation by postal subscription. The mail order habit is growing apace in this country and there is absolutely no reason why British publishers of women's magazines do not, and will not, expect to sell a useful and increasingly larger proportion of their total sales through the letter-box.

Donor subs are a big factor. A monthly magazine makes a wonderful present and, what is more, it will arrive 12 times instead of the one-off gift of flowers, or whatever. Most of the publishers currently concerned with subscriptions will send a gift card announcing the present and the donor is then fondly remembered every month for the next year. This builds up the magazine habit and if the gift ceases when the niece decides to send auntie a hair-brush next Christmas the publisher has a good on-going subscription candidate in auntie. And although a new subscriber may be converted from bookshop purchase, statistics prove that a vigorous and sensible subscription sales programme will create a definite numerical gain in sales. A year's subscription also guarantees that a buyer will buy 12 times and not desert the title by flirting with a contemporary magazine. Convential wisdom (rather loosely researched or proven) claims that a 'regular reader' will only buy 6 out of 12 issues of a monthly magazine.

We are firm believers in subscription selling. We have found it immediately successful. We mentioned subsidiary benefits, and these will be discovered with the free mailing list of subscribers at the publishers' disposal. It is easy to include a letter with the subscription copy selling some extra service to the subscriber – a special offer, a reader 'treat' and so on. *Country Living*, which has built up a very rapid subscription list, has even created the ambience of a special insider's club – Friends of Country Living – who are made to feel very special. This is a build-up of reader brand loyalty which is priceless. One of the great USPs of women's magazines is the one-to-one relationship between editor and reader and subscription loyalty is a classic example of how the relationship can be cemented. We are firmly of the opinion that a monthly women's magazine should not settle for less than 10 per cent of the UK circulation as subscriptions.

The wholesale and retail trade (not to mention the distributor) may whinge at this activity outside their sphere of influence (and their cash tills), but like supermarket sales it is the future and all this ancillary selling (ancillary to the trade) will help to expand the market to the eventual benefit of all.

Our enthusiasm for subscription selling, however, stops short of some of the more seductive and seemingly desperate methods of cut-price 'come-ons' which creep onto the market. Sometimes presents are offered as lures – a book, a diary, etc. These are passable selling techniques but have a dubious quality when renewals are due. Such offers invite the one-off purchase whereas the art form is to build up a more permanent relationship with the subscriber. Even worse, in our view, is the overt cut-price offers which have been seen around. *Vogue*,

The Tatler and *House & Garden* have been regularly offering 25 per cent discounts and the launch of *W* was accompanied by 40 per cent discounts. Such profligacy will undoubtedly and understandingly irritate the news trade, creating seemingly unfair competition.

We would add a rider or two when setting out to build subscriptions. They must be planned to arrive on the doormat on time, preferably just before, or at least coincidental with, publishing day. Subscribers get justifiably furious when they see their favourite magazine on sale in the local news agent before their copy has arrived in the post. And the copies must arrive in mint condition, in the excellent plastic envelopes which ensure flat delivery – bouncing back to the horizontal even when folded double by the postman.

It would be untrue to state that the postal deliveries in the UK are constantly and consistently conducive to punctual arrivals. But the Post Office will be under continual pressure from the interested publishers in treating magazines as a vital and lucrative commodity.

Perhaps the smaller, or tyro, publisher will look particularly at the subscription route because the pressure on newsstand space will continue to grow more acute. There are already signs of 'delisting' products, a practice long prevalent in the big supermarkets. It is only rational that a retailer can, and will, limit the numbers of computer titles or motoring magazines which he can sensibly (or even physically display). If the new launch ambition is to produce a magazine for a certain and identifiable sub-group, then it may be much more effective to build a subscription list and eschew the news trade route altogether. The fact is, it is more likely to eschew you.

Of course, the retailers and the wholesalers are going to get very choosy about the sheer multitude of titles which have been flooding the market. The big titles from the big publishing companies will continue to predominate and this will be at the expense of the more esoteric. So the only route, apart from the subscription one, might be free distribution as discussed in an earlier chapter. This entails a complete reliance on advertising income and that presents the smaller publisher with an entirely different problem.

Another distribution method which has lost some of its vitality in the past couple of decades has been home delivery. It was much more the custom in times past for a woman customer to have her favourite magazine delivered by the newsboy to her home. This had the decided advantage to the publisher and shopkeeper of regular ordering from the same sales point. Perhaps it started to decline when cover prices crept up in the 1970s, giving the customer a shock when presented with the newsbill. It may have also been due to the weight of magazines in the newsboy's satchel, but this does not seem to have caused crippling on a Sunday morning so far. Home delivery is a consummation devoutly to be wished and encouraged.

Every so often the cry goes up in the world of publishing to 'innovate'. Dispenser machines outside closed retail outlets, or sales at garages, or sports magazines in sports shops and knitting magazines in wool shops. These are all false scents, or certainly trivial ones. We have in this country a magnificent retail sector, easy access to most geographical points and a huge population crowded into our bulging island. The wholesale trade is steadily gearing itself up, cerebrally and mechanically, to a 'Brave New World' and the distribution companies are becoming very professional in their approach to marketing and merchandising. Fortunately the British are very fond of magazines, and women particularly so. As there are some 22 million women in our reader universe the whole circulation merry-go-round will continue to serve the publisher well. If an old-established magazine dies it will be because it has become terminally ill and reached the end of its tether. If a new launch fails to catch fire it will be because it was ill conceived or unwanted. It will not be the fault of the 'circulation trade'. This was very amply illustrated by the massive success of the launch of *Prima* in 1986 when a circulation of one million was achieved solely and completely through trade channels.

There are going to be crushing problems ahead for this diverse industry but of all the difficulties which lie ahead for the magazine publisher we feel that distribution will not by any means be the most crucial. If we produce the right magazines for the right audiences, constantly keeping the product timely and competitively lively, then the circulation business will, literally, deliver the goods.

EDITORIAL AND PRODUCTION

The great changes which are taking place in the women's magazine market, with the added extra dynamic of foreign competition, are reflected in the editorial pages. Editors are realising that the new input of professionally designed magazines, as well as the newspapers becoming, in many instances, more and more like magazines – with their women's and general features and specialist columns – are producing creative competition not dreamed of by their predecessors. The newspaper colour supplements, in their privileged position of host circulations, are another threat. The press world has never been so vibrant with professional writers, photographers and art departments. The editors have to realise that they must produce consumer satisfaction to retain their readers. Conventional wisdom says that half the readers are loyal and the other half are more transient: the editor's art is to satisfy this more fickle portion of their reader catchment. It's a delicate balancing act – to gain one new reader at the expense of an existing one is fruitless.

There has been a tendency in the past for an editor to write 'for herself'. Her magazine was aimed at the sort of person she was, as well as her friends. One glossy magazine editor considered that his circle of friends in Fulham was entirely representative of his half-million other readers. But successful magazines have to be targeted at market segments based on age and life-style, now considerably helped by profiles built up by the TGI and other surveys. The magazine has to deliver what the reader wants and expects. If it does not, there is always another magazine which produces the formula a reader likes.

As the magazines push each other off the bookstall in the battle for prominence, the front cover is the supreme selling tool. The cover picture, the colours, the cover lines – these are the art director's weapons against the competition. The cover will entice the buyer and identify with the reader. It's the supreme moment of sale. The philosophy of what makes a good cover would fill a chapter on its own but there is no doubt that a bright cover, with strong colours and lively cover lines which make a promise to the reader, are giving the magazine the best chance of leaving the bookshelf. The cover line which makes a promise which is then unfulfilled inside the magazine (common with cheaper paperbacks and some magazines) may lose a reader for ever.

The editor's image is firmly planted with the magazine, creating the ideal one-to-one ambience which all editors seek. The good editor, and her staff and contributors, must identify their readers, recognise their needs, never talk down to them and stay one jump ahead of them with new ideas. Equally, they must never go too far ahead of the reader so that she is alienated by the changes which race ahead of her own life-style. New editors will want to make changes in the product, but we have seen too many instances of a new editor, eyes glistening with the excitement of a new challenge, making drastic changes of direction which upset the old readership and fail to attract the new – certainly not in the time that the management feels is warranted by the expense generated.

Undoubtedly there are fashions in magazine editorial style and women's magazines do incline to be an imitative breed. Editors tend to live and work in the same sort of environment as each other, to go to the same press parties and launches, to have worked on each other's magazines and to employ some of the same contributors and staff as part of the merry-go-round. All this will create a certain sameness and, occasionally, a downright coincidence of features and interviews. There is an apocryphal story of the reader who wrote to a well-known weekly, after seeing on occasions not only similar features but similar covers: 'Dear madam, I love your magazine but why do you keep changing the title?'

The other editorial fashion is for more than one magazine to fall in love with the work of a particular journalist or photographer, which helps to create the look-alike syndrome. And other creative people, observing how much the original contributor seems to be used by the editors, will model their own work on the original – quickly helping to

140

create an editorial genre of which the editors *en masse* quickly tire.

Needless to say, it is the individuality and originality of a creative editor which helps the magazine to establish a strong self-identity and personality. Such a magazine will be a brand leader in these days of cut-throat competition. Imitation, the prosaic, the mundane and the 'passing off' will make for second-rate magazines and accelerate the fading away and ultimate death of the lesser titles. Each magazine has to find its true positioning, its 'branding' (in the marketeer's vernacular), to establish its place in the great magazine mix. It is a truism and a cliché to suggest that a magazine will only flourish if it provides the editorial which the targeted readership wants and needs, but that is a simple fact of life. A good editor does not necessarily ensure a successful magazine – there may be many other commercial factors working against it – but there is no doubt that a bad editor will hasten her title's departure – or her own.

Editors are stars and should be treated like stars. The big names in magazines are beginning to realise their worth and there is little doubt that their salaries will increase alongside the self-recognition of their status in the industry. Like all high-status jobs there is also high risk, and risk has to be paid for. As the media whirligig accelerates in pace and frenetic volatility the editor will be more and more vulnerable to management sensitivity. The boardroom will be more likely than ever to shoot the pianist when the melody is not to their satisfaction. On the other hand, the editor who gets it all very right will get the plaudits and the laurel wreath.

We asked several well-known and successful editors how they saw their own readerships and how they perceived their markets changing in the future – how their readers might themselves evolve in these fast-moving times and how their editorial stance might have to change as well.

Linda Kelsey, *Cosmopolitan*'s editor, said:

The Cosmo girl of the early '70s has evolved into a highly sophisticated young woman. Her major concerns are the same but her priorities are shifting in step with a fast-changing world. The girl who would have been content to share a rented flat has wised up to the money market and is busy paying off a mortgage. Having a career is no longer a feminist issue – it's a fact of life that most women expect to be working right up until retirement age, albeit with short-breaks for child-rearing.

Over the next few years *Cosmopolitan* will consolidate its position as the leading authority on young women with extended careers' coverage, money management features and greater emphasis on the fashion, food and life-style that our ever-more affluent readers will be able to afford. In the realm of relationships we will continue our uniquely in-depth, compassionate and humorous reflections on living and loving in the closing years of the twentieth century.

David Hepworth, editorial director of Emap Metro, who launched *Smash Hits* and *Just Seventeen* and has created Emap's *More!* said:

If the last 20 years of teenage magazine publishing have one thing to teach us it's that success tends to lie in recruiting new readers young and holding on to them for as long as possible. The competitors to worry about are rarely those addressing themselves to an older age bracket. *Just Seventeen*'s readers start at the age of 13 and hang on until they're 18 and over. While every factor surrounding the title – from the remorselessly advancing age of even its most fresh-faced staff to the peer pressure that looms over both writers and readers and the unspoken demands of advertisers – is tending to nudge it up the age/sophistication scale, the editors have to resist these trends and push the magazine younger in order to keep it in the same place. In this sense it seems that if you take the low ground you have the high ground.

Simultaneously there seems no reason to suppose that the age at which teenage attitudes are formed will not continue to get younger. It seems likely that tomorrow's teenager will not always be in her teens. This trend is driven by the lowering age of puberty and an increasing sophistication – albeit superficial – imparted by proliferating mass media.

While TV will continue to treat teenage girls as morons (when it can be bothered to treat them at all) and can only respond late to trends that start in dark corners of the youth sub-culture, teenage magazines like *Just Seventeen* can take part in the process that TV can only observe. What they must continue to do is minister to the desire for personality, idiosyncracy, romance and a little judicious rebellion. In this respect they will continue to court controversy by covering the subjects that some adults would rather they be shielded from.

And although we have to accept that we are in an increasingly image-driven society these publications have a crucial role to play in encouraging the habit of healthy scepticism as well as the habit of reading. The way things are going the latter already seems mildly subversive in itself.

Deirdre McSharry, the erstwhile *Cosmopolitan* editor who has moved to more bucolic pastures, is very positive about the *Country Living* reader:

142

The Yuppy, whose only reading matter was the Filofax, is dead. Killed by the Big Crash of October 1987. Long live the concerned, caring and articulate *reader* who wishes to be inspired as well as entertained. 'Enlightened self-interest' is the mood of the 650,000-plus readers of *Country Living* who face an uncertain future with quiet confidence. The woman's movement and the technological revolution have brought an independent, work-efficient world to reality. But when the door closes on a working day spent in an air-conditioned high rise block, humming with chattering computers and Fax machines, what the human spirit needs is refreshment and contrast. A retreat from the dirt and pressure of urban society. An oasis where the fine things in life can be cherished. A world where ideas are discussed, books are read, gardens tended and houses lovingly decorated. A refuge where kitchens smell of gingerbread, dogs loll on sofas, silver is polished, linen is starched, herbs are dried and people care enough to belong and work for the local community, whether what they call 'the village' is actually Camden Town or Chipping Sodbury. It's the world of *Country Living* which has more to do with attitudes than geography. In less than two years *Country Living* has captured the high ground of this spiritual country for a readership that demands more from life than getting and spending. Like all successful magazines this one charts a love affair. And the love affair is timeless and endless because the loved one is the mythical countryside we all long to inhabit. It's Wordsworth country, Laurie Lee country as well as the countryside of the National Trust, Laura Ashley and Knight, Frank & Rutley. With their concern for conserving and handing on our greatest national asset, the countryside and its houses, our readers are the true pioneers, the real leaders of the 1990s.

Judith Hall, the editor of IPC's *Woman's Weekly*, is prescient about the ever-growing army of the greying:

Britain's best-selling magazine is not the brashest, the glossiest or the most action-packed. It's the one that, in the words of so many *Woman's Weekly* readers, 'comes into the home each week like a friend'. The magazine *is* friendly and unashamedly homely, and therein, I think, lies its success: in a changing, and sometimes bewildering world, *Woman's Weekly* has been a touchstone of security for generations of women. The sort of women who, in the sixties, were made to feel like cabbages by the rest of the media because home was where their heart was and they didn't *want* to sleep around; but *Woman's Weekly* was there to let them know that they weren't alone – whatever the headlines might say, millions of women were just like them. What I find fascinating is that *Woman's Weekly* has held rock-steady to its values, while the world has gravitated back to its way of thinking: in the late eighties, the basic Christian principles – of fidelity and faith,

143

unworldly wisdom and the work ethic, even hand-knitteds and home bakes – are right back in fashion.

The rest of this decade and the next are, I think, going to witness the ever-rising profile of the older market – and *Woman's Weekly* will be up there in the vanguard. The average age of our readers is 50 and, far from camouflaging the fact, I intend to celebrate it. 'Retirement' is a ghastly word, with its intimations of the long goodbye – 'self-hood', I'd say, is a better thought. The children have left home, the mortgage is paid off, maybe the insurance policy has paid out. Duty done, you've the time to rediscover yourself (and, if you're lucky, himself) and, chances are, the money to indulge yourself too. That's what my readers are telling me, and *Woman's Weekly* is with them all the way. The advertisers will cotton on, in time: when they wake up to the fact that it's possible to be glad to be grey – and have spending power. . . .

Jill Churchill, the editor of International Thomson's *Family Circle*, writes:

Family Circle is perhaps fortunate in its title. Certainly we seem to be at a point in time when women are 'thinking family' more than at any decade since the magazine's launch in the 1960s. I believe that this may be partly force of circumstances – the economy of the 80s has certainly directed many would-be career women into the paths of domesticity. But there is also a detectable emotional swing away from the 'me generation' so vaunted in the 70s.

So while my reader may be a somewhat reluctant housewife, waiting out her time until the economic climate improves, she is by no means averse to the word 'family'. With family comes importance, a managerial need for enterprise and expertise; with education, health, financial planning high on the agenda. Meanwhile there is the ever-present need to cook and clean, shop and sew – so my reader demands ever more stimulating ideas, recipes, information, in all the home-based areas.

But of course it is hard to generalise about a readership as large as *Family Circle*'s (currently the largest of any women's monthly in Britain). Some of my readers are widows of 60, others are nineteen-year-old brides. Despite the 'new' trends detected above, I believe one strand remains constant through the decades and may indeed be stronger than ever today. I refer to the comparative loneliness of the reader.

It was with this loneliness in mind that I decided to put a strong emphasis on 'peopling' the magazine when I took over the editorship in 1982. We regularly publish reports from our unique 'Reader's Register' of volunteers who double-test all our recipes, our knitting patterns and our d-i-y makes; we carry stories of fellow women who have lived through experiences that may inspire others; and we run celebrity interviews that emphasise, not sensationalism, but rather the commonality of interests that may be shared between the famous and the much-maligned 'Mrs Average'.

Perhaps the best demonstration of this 'peopling' was the decision in 1982 to – literally – give the magazine a human face. Before then it was customary to carry food photography on the cover. Then we decided to go for 'real women'. From then on we achieved ten successive circulation increases.

As for my claim that my readers 'think family' – this is borne out by our continuous research (again started in 1982) which showed me, eventually, that I could not carry enough child-related features to meet the reader's needs without overbalancing the general mix of the magazine. My answer had to be to launch a satellite magazine – *Practical Parenting* – under the *Family Circle* banner. Piloted in 1987, it met a sufficiently enthusiastic response to become a regular monthly publication in 1988.

Sue Dobson, editor of *Woman and Home*, comments

The great thing about *Woman and Home* readers is that they know what they want! Having survived the worst insecurities of the teens and twenties, they understand themselves, know their own values, needs and interests, and have more time (and money) to spend on the things they enjoy doing. Keen cooks, they want innovative recipes for good, and preferably healthy, food, and especially appreciate menus for entertaining; interested in their homes, they look for stylish ideas in decor and crafts. They enjoy doing complicated knitting patterns, want well-written fiction and like to read about interesting people and places. They look to their magazine to be practical, creative, informative and entertaining – and, as in everything they buy, they demand value for money.

Finally, we asked Sue James, the editor of *Prima*, for her analysis of Prima Woman. As there are one million of them, produced out of a publishing hat in such a surprisingly short space of time, it is interesting to read her comments. Rival publishers will discover no magic elixir:

Defining a magazine's ideal reader is every editor's first job. For me it was easy and in a very short space of time I have got to know a lot about the women who buy *Prima*. Women have come a long way in the last ten years and what comes across strongly is the new confidence they have in their wide-ranging role. For that reason they want a magazine that satisfies their every mood.

Our *Prima* reader is practical – she has to be! She probably has a house to look after, [is] married with a family to care for, a budget to balance and most often has a job too. No mean feat. She is creative, she's a doer, she likes the fact that *Prima* offers options that are accessible and encouraging. She wants to be stylish but not outrageous, informed and entertained. The surprising thing is that there is not an archetypal *Prima* woman – she could be any one of us, come from any walk of life and be of any age. But what all *Prima* readers have in common is an intelligent and realistic approach to life today as it concerns them and their families.

Their interests cover the full range of classic women's topics – fashion and beauty, homecraft and homestyle, knitting and dressmaking, traditional and innovative cookery, plus a whole host of general features on family health, consumer advice, travel, pets and gardening; all part of the *Prima* editorial approach which is always friendly and never condescending.

In fact, there's nothing particularly unusual about the *Prima* woman – she's like most other women today and yesterday. But today, she has the determination to structure and enjoy her life in the way she chooses.

After the rather heady reader analysis and prognostications of this distinguished gathering of editors we turn to the equally prophetic subject of print and paper. Production is the key to absolutely everything else in the world of magazines. What the newspapers call 'new technology' has been around the magazine business for a long time. We asked Brian Boddy, the production director of the National Magazine Company, for his views on what is going to happen:

The division between 'creation' and 'manufacture' in the Pre-press of activity will become more and more obscure as we approach the end of the century. It is within this area of activity [that] there has been significant development which will continue at an even faster pace in the future.

Desk top personal computers have created the means whereby the creative writer and the designer can interpret electronically their words and designs. Available software can give the writer the facility to describe in typographic terms the typeface, size, leading and line width. More sophisticated packages enable the art director to manipulate the text into made-up pages and if a laser printer is available to output camera ready copy. Alternatively, the disc containing the text and page layout structure may be used to generate film from a typesetter.

From the desk top there is the resource of the composing room. All of this is available now and undoubtedly development will continue apace especially in the area of desk top scanners. Scanning of mono tone pictorial subjects is available now, however the quality, while being to a reasonable standard, has and will be improved.

Design work stations enabling the designer to create a layout including colour originals, tinted lettering and panels as well as incorporating text will be more widely used. One of the deterrent factors at present is not the technology but the price. As software houses who are independent of the graphics industry become more involved in developing software systems I am convinced that the price will become more realistic. Desk top publishing is a pointer in this direction whereby pages of text and mono originals can be made up on screen and output via a laser printer, the cost of the software being well within the financial resources of the smallest publisher. While pages will be designed on screen at the publisher's the scanning of colour will remain, for the foreseeable future, the domain of the professional repro house. Electronic layouts from the publisher will be used as the matrix into which scanned material will be drawn. No more the arguments of the repro house positioning or masking incorrectly; the electronic layout created by the publisher is the means of obtaining position and size.

Proofing, that ages-old insurance that the villainous supplier has not totally destroyed the content or aesthetism of the design, will change dramatically. The horse-and-cart element of conveying paper or other such substrate between supplier and publisher will eventually disappear to be replaced by the electronic proof. Typematter and mono tone originals will be generated in the publisher's office via a laser printer from the supplier with corrections keyed at a work station and transmitted back to the supplier. Colour pages will be seen at a colour work station, again generated from the supplier with the option of producing a hard copy proof in colour via a laser or ink jet printer. Corrections to layout and possibly colour correction may be carried out at this stage.

My opening comments were related to the disappearing division between creative input and manufacturing. Should the predictions above come to be, and many are now in being or are in development, then the skills of our editorial personnel of the future will be very different.

Creation of the image carrier, whether it be gravure cylinder or litho plate, will become totally filmless. In fact, this is now becoming more and more a reality in gravure where engraving is controlled by data input rather than by scanning hard copy. With the introduction of electron beam engraving before the end of the century, capable of engraving at speeds of 150,000 cells per second, only electronically transmitted data is capable of supporting the system. Creation of litho plates without film will be developed by-passing the necessity of generating film from the scanner and planning the material prior to plate manufacture.

Press speeds continue to increase with web offset presses running in

147

excess of 600 metres per minute which on a two round press converts to just in excess of 900 revolutions of 50,000 copies per hour. Gravure speed are approximately the same – however the number of pages printed at a press pass are considerably more than litho at these speeds. Gravure presses with a cylinder width of 3 metres are now in production capable of producing up to 120 pages at one press pass. Reels weighing up to 4–5 tonnes are required to feed these monster presses, even so a reel change will occur every 12 minutes. Press speeds are of course governed by the paper weight passing through the press.

Development will be in the area of press make-ready times with the emphasis on faster turn-round between sections, which in turn will provide more efficient use of the most important raw material, paper.

Demand for paper and particularly coated grades will continue to rise. Forecasts of additional capacity in the light weight coated area of manufacture to 1990 is 1,350,000 tonnes. Based on the past 10 years' growth this capacity will be absorbed into the market. While I do not believe there will be a shortage of coated grades neither will there be a glut. The coated mechanical market will divide into two grades, namely, single coated and double coated. This trend is beginning with the up-market glossy titles utilising the double coated grade. More mills will change over to this grade giving publishers a wider choice starting at 70 gsm and upward. There will be a considerable demand for the single coated grades unless of course it is phased out leaving only double coated grade to satisfy this market, in which case premiums will also have to be phased out.

Pigmentised papers will continue to grow as developments improve the quality. They may even fill the gap in what is now the single coated mechanical market, especially if single coated is phased out toward the end of the 1990s.

As a final thought consider the integration of the made-up page data with advanced laser or ink jet printers capable of four-colour reproduction. Printing of multi-page products quickly and efficiently at any number of remote stations without the requirement of creating an image carrier becomes a possibility!

THE STATE OF THE ART

If we have to sum up the most significant development in women's magazine publishing since the early 1980s it has to be the emergence of the continental publishers, with their vast resources and voracious print capacity, on to the UK market. The very successful launch of *Prima* in the autumn of 1986 came like an ice-cold douche on the heads of many British publishing executives, to be followed in less than a year by the weekly *Best* from the same publishers. As we write the continentals are queueing up with their ideas and although some will probably never see the light of day the floodgates have been seen to be openable.

The effect and efficiency of the continental invasion will go on rumbling for a long time – indeed the British magazine market will never be the same again. When the initial shock waves have passed (and they will probably be renewed with each new launch), we will be able to assess the benefits and disadvantages of their new energy pumped into our market. There is no doubt that the sheer speed of the build-up to one million monthly sales was breathtaking and the impact of *Best* on the weekly market, hitherto the almost exclusive domain of IPC, has altered the balance of power. But more far-reaching even than the successful Panzer attack was the editorial formula. The Teutonic watershed was even more surprising by its conviction that what the British reading public wanted was (a) a return to crafts and almost cosy *hausfrau* activities, and (b) short, sharp stories which cut reading time to a minimum. There seems little doubt that both these seemingly correct beliefs will have a strong editorial influence on existing and future women's titles.

So we can foresee that this technique will be emulated, that other mass launches are inevitable, that the death of some other titles will be hastened, that competition will get fiercer, and publishers will have to revaluate the cost of launches. There was much talk in the trade press at the time of the launch of the German magazines about 'moving the goal posts', a reference to the much longer period waiting for an actual profit than is the custom exercised by British companies. Gruhner & Jahr have been quoted as being satisfied with a seven-year pay-back period, being content to build up a solid circulation base and allowing the advertising to catch up. Indeed, the first issues of *Best* and *Bella* had few advertisements. This is almost a mirror reflection of the established viewpoint that advertising has to be virtually guaranteed before embarking on the cold waters of a launch. The German invasion had twin motives – first, to establish a bridgehead in the lucrative British market which seemed to them to be full of gaps and, second, because they had hungry printing presses and a profligacy of women's titles back home.

We must not get obsessed that the continental invasion refers only to Germany. The Netherlands has the massive VNU, very vigorous in the women's market, and Italy cannot be ignored. The Americans, outside the confines of Hearst, Condé Nast and the international news magazines may also find their appetites whetted. This will certainly apply to Murdoch.

The other overt development will be the vogue for global publishing where the boardrooms throughout the world will see the attractions and possibilities of extending their boundaries. Of course, *Reader's Digest*, *Time-Life* and *Newsweek* have always seen the world as their oyster and Hearst and Condé Nast have polished the technique to a fine art. *Good Housekeeping* was launched in the USA in 1885 and came to Britain in 1922, followed by *Harper's Bazaar* in 1929. *Cosmopolitan* was an explosion of licensing efficiency when Hearst appreciated that the Helen Gurley Brown formula born in 1964 was eminently exportable. When the British version proved so sensationally successful they swiftly followed up by selling the license in South America, Japan, The Netherlands, France, Italy, Germany, Australia, South Africa, Greece and Hong Kong. Even such a seemingly indigenous product as *Country Living* has been transformed with great success to Britain and Australia. *Good Housekeeping* has its Japanese, Australian and South American versions. Condé Nast have followed the route of establishing their own satellite companies in foreign climes with *Vogue* and *House & Garden* in various editions. Murdoch has seen the possibilities with *Elle* and will slowly but surely expand that title in strategic parts of the globe. Their ambitions seem endless, with mention of editions as far apart as Japan, Saudi Arabia, Hong Kong and the USSR.

But the rest of the world of publishing, in the global sense of the phrase, will not stand idly by. The years of 1986 and 1987 saw a plethora of new titles breaking out. Finland launched *Gloria*, France *Alma*, *Maxi*, *Paris Joyce* and *Jeune et Jolie*, Germany *Flying Dutchman*, *Lady* and *Playgirl*, Holland *Yes*, Spain *Mia* and Belgium *Elga*, *Flair* and a senior citizens magazine called *Notre Temps*, Who can say when some of these titles may appear in British versions?

The British market will show a net expansion with foreign intervention. *Prima* increased figures of the entire ABC market by some 3 per cent in the first half of 1987 and the fast-moving weeklies, present or future, will surely add to the expansion. The weekly market itself baffles the art of prediction. We have already eaten humble pie by confessing our incorrect prognostication about this part of the market, given that *Best* will continue to sell a million and other entrants will arrive. Somebody has forecast that the desired million is not necessarily a yardstick – that the market in the 1990s may consist of a variety of titles all selling about 600,000 and all thereby being profitable. The key to so much of the momentum of the weekly market has to be IPC, and our previous gloom about the future of the weeklies was encouraged by Gerry Wynveldt, erstwhile managing director of IPC's circulation company, when he forecast in 1983 the eventual death of the weeklies. This was no casual remark – it was actually made at the 1983 Autumn Magsell presentation when Mr Wynveldt suggested that the weekly titles had a mere 25 years' life-span ahead of them. This statement was received frostily by the IPC management, swiftly followed by the removal of the forecaster from IPC. We ourselves are now more cheery that the weeklies will survive and prosper, but we feel that the market will indeed have to be satisfied with smaller circulations, several more titles and a change in editorial techniques.

The weeklies will, by definition, continue to use broad brush-strokes while the monthlies will offer more specialised readerships. 'Niche publishing' will be the watchword. *Prima* is, in this context, specialised because it appeals to the 'do' side of the female nature. (It also presents its fashion pages like a mail order catalogue with the clothes clearly and explicitly photographed. Too many women's magazines allow the fashion editor her flights of fancy with her choice of photographer, price levels and ambiguous pictures. Although this may suit some of the esoteric glossies it clearly does not appeal to the middle ground which the Germans have exploited.) But there is niche and niche.

Working Woman was the niche that wasn't. Ignore the comedy of errors of the fortunes of the various owners – the market which they sought was soggy ground. It is interesting to read Audrey Slaughter's introduction to the Women's Interest section of the useful and comprehensive *Magazine Distribution Book* for spring/summer 1985: 'Magazines must move and adapt to social change. Now that women aren't all stirring a stock pot on the back of a stove, worrying about the whites of their washing, the purely domestic magazines must appeal to an ever-decreasing number.' We totally agree with her first sentence but doubt if the second is entirely accurate. There is undoubtedly and obviously a new breed of working woman, anticipated by so many magazines of the 1970s and the early 1980s, and their needs and interests are being reflected in the positive changes in all women's magazines. Even *Prima* recognises the working status in their formula but equally so the domestic energy and satisfaction that women may get from the domestic side of their often Jekyll and Hyde existence. This is perhaps why *Working Woman* was too blatant an approach and as difficult to isolate as a magazine called 'Working Man'.

The reader, and the advertiser, will be looking for value for money in the magazines which go on surviving to the end of the century. Cover mounts will continue to be popular 'down market' and there will inevitably be a preponderance of banded supplements and other extras. The advertiser will remain interested in regional editions, now run by several titles and a host of 'widgets' which print technology can produce will be seen more and more. Advertisement promotions will be a major selling extra for the up-market monthlies because they are sales effective for the advertisers, but we suspect that their identification within the magazine will have to be more precise.

Who is going to read women's magazines? Although the universe is growing the gross readership of NRS titles is falling.

Try to com

Table 1a: Gross readership of titles covered by NRS

	(Adults, millions)						
Population	37,000*	38,600*	40,100	41,300	43,150	44,000	44,650
Index	100	104	108	112	117	119	121
	1956	1961	1966	1971	1981	1986	1987
Women's Weeklies	43.8	50.2	38.2	35.4	30.7	24.4	23.9
Women's Monthlies	35.3	34.0	30.0	43.7	40.9	39.6	39.1

*Sixteen and over, 15 and over remainder.
Source: National Readership Survey.

If we look at the percentage proportion of women reading any women's monthly the picture is clear.

Table 1b

Women (000s)	22,378	22,448	22,518	22,696	22,960	23,055	23,095	23,200
Index	100	100	101	101	103	103	103	104
	1980	1981	1982	1983	1984	1985	1986	1987
	50	48	45	44	47	46	45	45

1986 and 1987 figures, 12 months to June.
Source: NRS.

The table can be read two ways. Although 45 per cent of adult women are reading a women's monthly, 55 per cent are not and should be very much a target area for new titles, because obviously the existing titles are not of interest to them. This is, of course, a simplistic view but does indicate that the market is there to be expanded. Where will this expansion come from?

There is one preoccupation which will undoubtedly spawn new titles and bolster up the profits of existing ones: the home. Magazines devoted to hearth and home are as popular and as varied as they were 100 years ago. The classics like *Ideal Home, Family Circle, Woman & Home, Homes & Gardens, House & Garden, Home & Freezer Digest* have been joined by the foodies (*Taste, A la Carte, Cooks Weekly*) and the very closely targeted *Country Living* and *Country Homes & Interiors*. The stratosphere is covered by the *World of Interiors* and the lifestyle by *Good Housekeeping* and *Options*. Splinter groups are setting up, like *Traditional Homes*. It is all ideal magazine territory and the titles have satisfactorily reflected the social changes.

The new baby boom may be seen by some apparently prescient publisher to be another lucrative area for expansion but the market has so far remained unresponsive. *Mother*, *Mother & Baby* and *Parents* 'work the hall' with sporadic one-shots appearing but, rather in the fashion of the health and exercise boomlet of the late 1970s, the subject will be taken up by the weeklies and the monthlies as and when they wish.

However much the older titles (in the establishment and reader profile senses), tend to consolidate their success, there will continue to be the customary zigzags on the graphs of births and deaths in the teenage and younger women's markets. IPC have sold their comics to Mr Maxwell and certainly seem to be less interested in the teeny-bopper (if the phrase is still in the currency) market. After all the violent deaths, and painful births, of the 1950s and 1960s this part of the market is more stable. Argus still have their romantic three (*True Romances*, *True Story* and *Woman's Story*) which they are actively marketing as a single buy to advertisers. D. C. Thomson have their Feminine Three with *Red Letter*, *Secrets* and *My Weekly*. All have seen serious circulation decline and perhaps *Chat* and *Celebrity* are more to the current taste. Thomsons also have their *Jackie*, *Blue Jeans* and *Patches* which, too, have declined in circulation over the years. Emap's *Smash Hits* and *Just Seventeen*, remarkable for their editorial energy and active graphics, have really changed the market. But this has always been a volatile group and the changing tastes of the generations, currently so preoccupied with music, may engineer further about turns. The older generation of titles, in comparative terms, is still dominated by *Cosmopolitan* which sits in a circulation and advertising volume head and shoulders over the competition. *Honey* has gone and *Look Now* and *Over 21* are surviving on the outer edge. *Woman's World* and *Company* have maintained their position but will be assailed by *Elle* and Emap's entrant for the first time into the age group, *More!*; *19* has shown signs of recuperation having swallowed *Honey*. There will obviously be continued publisher interest in this young market, even though the group is suffering from a population fade. It is interesting to recall the table

Table 2

	Teenagers	Freedom years	Independent young mothers	Young matrons
	15–19	20–24	25–29	30–34
	000s	000s	000s	000s
1979	1,900	1,710	1,670	1,790
1981	1,960	1,780	1,640	1,820
1986	1,860	1,950	1,770	1,620
1991	1,540	1,860	1,940	1,760

Source: Whitehead Report on Population Trends.

published as part of the Whitehead Report on Circulation Trends in the late 1970s to put the age groups in perspective.

The 15–24s are a diminishing sector but it is pertinent to note that *Just Seventeen* has not suffered from this decline in its target audience, probably illustrating that the medium really *is* the message.

Will the regions play a more important role in the future? In our earlier book we discussed the emergence of a group of magazines expanding under the classification 'Special Interest Regional Magazines', geographically focused, specialised titles fast growing in the areas of sport, business, home interest and women. We drew attention to the existence of *Oklahoma Woman*, *Carolina Woman* and the launch of *Texas Woman*. We discussed the possibilities of the concept and suggested that, even with the limitations of circulation among the population in specific areas, the emergence of a magazine called *Yorkshire Woman* or *Scots Woman* would not be absolutely ruled out of court. We said that such a specialisation might be with us in the 1980s. It is satisfying to note that in the autumn of 1987 a husband and wife team launched *Wessex Woman*, a 90p bi-monthly glossy aiming at Wessex, with its geographical boundaries defined as Exeter and Cheltenham down to the Isle of Wight. 'All the popular women's magazines are far too London orientated and it is our aim to shift that emphasis to Wessex only' said one of the proprietors. The launch of *Frills* in late 1987 was defiantly produced from Birmingham, albeit seeking a national circulation, and endeavouring to bring a regional flavour to its editorial return to romantic frippery.

We can also record the entry of *Birmingham Woman*, *Fenestra* (Fashion–Sheffield), *Lady Gossip* from Altrincham and *New Warwickshire Woman*.

Cover prices will continue to rise, even if at not more than the rate of inflation and the probable introducton of VAT. Publishers are not as chary as they used to be about price increases, having seen several titles taking the bit between their teeth and prospering. World paper prices continue to be aggressive and the cost of production of magazines will never catch up with the possible market price of the titles on the bookstalls.

Magazines will continue to evolve to suit their advertisers as much as their readers, although no judicious editor would beam her magazine overtly towards the advertiser. The advertiser will follow the readership built up by the successful magazine and the nuances of change in the life-style of the woman reader are also the changes sought by the advertiser. The fact that over 38 per cent of all women are working will be reflected by the magazines, as will the facts of life that women are better educated, have better jobs, smaller families, more disposable income, more freedom, greater purchasing power and much wider lives than their mothers did. A growing number of women live on their own, or as the heads of single-parent families, with a financial and sexual freedom which creates (or has been created by) a wholly different magazine ethos.

Advertisers will alter their attitudes to women and in the past decade this has become obvious.

Obviously the home will continue to dominate in women's advertising but with a new dimension. The choice of goods, materials and services will become more unisex as the domestic jobs are shared. The gardening, decorating and minor electrical repairs will not necessarily be as sexually divided as once they were, and the advertiser of appropriate goods will want to reach both parties. This probably already happens in many homes, certainly when the cost is heavy, as with most consumer durables. Motor cars will become an even more important category – women will be the prime target for small cars, either the younger woman's first Mini or the family's second car. Financial services and institutions will also begin to accept, albeit slowly, that women are going to be more and more a separate and vital market segment.

In the USA there is already great emphasis on the woman as a target for corporate advertising and as a business user of airlines and hotels.

The day is coming when women will be able to consider buying themselves goods in the luxury class. Fur coats, diamonds and expensive jewellery will be seen as attainable prerequisites by the younger and middle-aged business woman and working wife.

Women car buyers will also need to purchase their own car insurance, and will be in the market for home and life insurance; these are areas which are largely ignored today by the big companies. Women – as single people, heads of one-parent families or wage-earning partners –are going to be increasingly segmented as a very real market force – and in countless different areas they represent a virtually untapped market.

The battle for the magazine share of the advertising pool will always be sharp. Magazine has to fight magazine, magazines have to fight newspapers and their colour supplements and magazines have to fight the electronic media. More television channels will be introduced as well as cable and satellite television. Commercial radio is beginning to grab more advertising share. Magazines have some specific advantages:

1. The advertiser can reach a more defined market than TV. From 100 titles any part of the vast audience can be segmented.
2. Pass-on readership is considerable.
3. Magazines give detailed information which can be kept for reference.
4. Magazines can accommodate loose inserts, bound-in inserts and coupons for direct response.
5. Some specialised magazines can provide selective national audiences.
6. The reader can choose the time she wants to sit and read. She can also spend as much time as she likes looking, as against TV or radio's instant and fleeting exposure.

It is engaging to recall a coincidence of the early 1980s, when two of us in the magazine publishing business hit upon the same happy contrivance by chance. We both imagined, in different public utterances, the state of the advertising world if electronic media had been around for centuries and some latter-day Gutenburg had suddenly discovered print. Our fellow-hallucinator was Michael Mander, then running International Thomson's magazines, and as his reverie was the more elegant it is eminently quotable here:

Indeed, we invited people to consider, if they had lived with electronic media only for 200 years, and magazines and press were suddenly invented today, with what excitement such an invention would be greeted.

(a) *At last* a medium where the speed of information transfer is dictated *not* by the medium, but by *the user*, who can skim and skip, absorb, stop, go back and jump ahead.

(b) *At last* a medium where information can be transferred quickly as people can read and absorb from *2 to 5 times faster* than they can listen.

(c) *At last* a *fully portable* medium, as easily used in a plane, or train, in the office or in bed, and needing *no installation or equipment*.

(d) *At last* a medium where complex and subtle advertising messages can be communicated.

(e) *At last* a medium where both the editorial and the advertisement content is relatively cheap to produce.

(f) a *flexible* medium giving an almost infinite permutation of audiences. And a medium virtually free of legislation, control by quango, licence or franchise.

(g) a tangible medium, with coupons and order forms.

Research will play an increasing part in the function of launching and selling advertising in magazines. This research will by necessity be qualitative as it is quality which distinguishes magazine from magazine and magazine from broadcast. As Joe Hanson, editor of the magazine *Folio*, says:

> To begin with, evaluating magazines strictly on a quantitative basis fails to recognise the essential difference between magazines and broadcast as advertising media. Broadcast delivers numbers. Magazines deliver readers. The act of reading involves an exchange of information and ideas that make advertising work differently in magazines [from] in broadcast.

Rate cutting

Probably the other most vexing problem to agitate and disturb magazine publishers, if we establish the continental invasion as the premier one, is the menace of rate cutting and rate discounting. Magazine publishers will have heavily and distinctly to brand their positions if we are not to be lumped together as a commodity purchase. To cut the rate is the sign of a weak or ailing medium and, once a rate is cut, there is no way that the advertiser or the media buyer is going to allow that rate to be restored to commercial normality. Of course, some magazines will cut rates to survive and win battles against competitors but it is a downward slope, very slippery and probably fatal. The big successful branded magazine with the readership which the advertiser wants will stand firm, ignore the blandishments of the media departments and disregard the piratical forages of the down-market newspapers and the monopolistic electronic media. Magazines will, of course, have to offer value, and by sticking to value will survive and prosper. John Mack Carter, in one of his regular columns in the American trade magazine *Adweek* emphasises the magazine case in August 1985:

Understanding the value of value
Although specific examples are hard to come by – and all of us profess innocence – rumors of magazine advertising rate cutting continue to float in the air like pollen. To reduce sneezing, try these words from Marsteller Inc.:

'The person who first said, "I can get it for you wholesale" set salesmanship back 20 years by putting a curse on the value of selling value. As a result, "value" is a most misunderstood word.

'The best definition we can find goes like this: Value is the lowest overall price that must be paid to have a useful function or service performed reliably. Expressed another way, it's PV + AV = TV; or product value plus added value equals total value.

'There's a value in selling value: Buyers learn to look beyond the price itself. They learn that even if the products seem the same, Supplier A is almost never the same as Supplier B. They also learn that seldom can you buy value from the person with the special deal, or from the price cutter or the cut-rate merchandiser.'

You still get what you pay for.

Back in the 1920s William Randolph Hearst, the founder and proprietor of the already powerful Hearst newspaper and magazine empire, issued a declaration of principles to the advertisement departments. As part of a welter of instructions these words of wisdom ring down the decades:

Our newspapers must sell advertising only by their printed rate card. If your rate card is wrong, change it. If it is right, live up to every letter of it. There should be no double standard of morality involving buyer and seller of advertising. Cut rates, special concessions and secret rebates are boomerangs, which return to cripple progress when they are least expected. Men who make 'gentlemen's agreements' are not wanted.

> When position is demanded for advertisements, we must demand that position rates are paid. People who prefer the extra advantage of Pullman cars are willing to pay for this privilege. In the make-up of the paper, preference should be given to those advertisements which lend prestige and dignity to the advertising columns of our newspaper.

The realisation is that the magazine industry could destroy itself if the foolishness of rate discounting is allowed to take an insidious hold. Price erosion will in turn erode those very products which in the interests of the advertiser and agent should flourish and prosper. The magazine which is profitable will reinvest in the editorial products, making the magazine more attractive to more readers, and hence to the advertiser. The magazine which is eroding its own price structure is not going to have the financial elbow room to improve the editorial and production of the product and the spiral will go downward to the doom and death of the publication. The standard must be set by the successful titles – in a perfect world the biggest companies would issue iron rate cards to their staff and not weaken when other, and lesser, competitors get away with the advertising the market leaders would like to carry because they have bought their way on to the schedule. The magazine business will certainly be the loser when titles die but so will the advertising industry. The arguments for rate strength are unambivalent.

We shall continue to see a continual stream of new launches in the business of women's magazines. As we have seen, it is an industry which is always restless and innovative, constantly shedding and renewing its skin like a snake. New launches are not the sign of weakness of an ailing trade, rather are they the manifestation of a dynamic creative energy. Titles will die, some with short bursts of life and some after a considerable history but the life-cycle, long or short, applies to magazines as it does to the animal kingdom. Magazines will continue to be attractive to the entrepreneurial mind of the publisher, corporate or individual, because:

1. Magazines are a free market. No licence or franchise is needed as in the electronic media.
2. The new technology, ever evolving, can be allied to magazine production at all levels.
3. The wholesale and retail distribution network is available to all,

within certain limits, and welcomes the publishers' energy.
4. No vast labour forces are required, nor printing plants.
5. Magazines can be very profitable.
6. Magazines provide opportunities for profitable spin-offs, books, offers, cassettes, etc.
7. A very professional and experienced editorial and business workforce exists. They love new magazines!

We do not foresee protracted deathbed scenes of titles, old or new. The elephantine costs of running existing magazines, or launching new ones, will force publishers to make fast decisions about the viability of their products and swift action will have to be taken to minimise the effect of an obvious loss-maker. The bottom line will dictate over sentimentality or false hope. A magazine will have to pay its way in the cruel world of advertising and marketing. It will be an uphill slog for the winners of the game, but a prosperous one. We foresee not fewer launches but more in the restless search for the magazine gold-mine. We see less rate discounting, more marketing and research and, above all, a highly professional workforce which will move around the business increasingly as their value is recognised by the publishing companies.

Magazines do not operate in a media vacuum and the outside world of competition will make magazine publishing a very professional occupation, requiring nerve and intuition. Electronic media will inevitably expand as the century draws to a close and the world of newspapers, with its recently discovered use of 'new' technology, colour printing and sanity with its labour relations, will prove increasingly competitive to magazines. Not only will newspapers become more and more like magazines – scooped as news media by the immediacy of the electronic media – but those magazine-like features will beam closer and closer to their women readers in their hungry quest for advertising money. Nor, again, do we see any lack of interest in retail stores producing magazines for their own catchments of customers. These 'magazines' were once called catalogues. But as the lady of the house is showered with free drops of magazine look-alikes, a supply of Sunday supplements and an avalanche of radio, television, cable and satellite, the frowns of the magazine publishers may deepen.

But magazines will prevail as a medium. We do not view the enormous vicissitudes of the 1970s and the 1980s, with all those launches, deaths and sweeping changes, as women's publishers' Big Bang, to be followed with a market collapse and an eventual shake-out. There has been no Big Bang, just an exciting series of explosive events to make the business of publishing women's magazines the most enthralling and exciting in all the mêlée of the media.

Postscript

As we go to press the business of women's magazines is gyrating faster and faster. *Essentials* has been sucessfully launched by IPC and the third print order exceeded one million copies. Obviously an eyeball to eyeball with *Prima* is on the agenda. The BBC have entered the fray with the announcement of *The Clothes Show Magazine*, a spin-off from their successful eponymous television programme. IPC cried 'foul', voicing the opinion that such a venture out of a public monopoly represented unfair competition to the commercial magazine industry.

Murdoch magazines enter the fray with their British edition of *New Woman* with Frankie McGowan as editor and a settle-down circulation expectation of 225,000. *Marie Claire*'s launch date has been set at August and IPC are still sniffing around the graveside of *Nova* to see if they can arrange a resurrection of the body in 1989., Carlton Publishing played a surprise card with the announcement of *Riva*, a glossy 350,000 weekly aimed at ABC1 women aged 20 to 40. They aimed to combine the style and quality of a monthly with the pace and immediacy of a weekly. The title seemed to be meaningless but observers noted darkly that it had a continental tang. In the meantime *Options* would carry a supplement called *Notions*. Emap were on stream with *More!* and *Burda* in Germany were still suggesting that they might launch their *Carina* on the British market.

In the USA a senior citizen called Frances Lear produced a magazine for 50 plus women called *Lear* – 'a magazine for the woman who wasn't born yesterday.' It was claimed to be a sell out of the 470,000 print run and Ms Lear was reported to be planning a British edition. And late, late news was that *A la Carte* folded its tablecloth and died.

Appendix I

Mergers

The following appendix shows existing magazines into which other titles have been merged over the years. Sometimes the merged titles were married into each other first but we have simplified the stories by giving the dates of the death of the merged magazines. Their bones are, however, often interred in the living titles.

EXISTING TITLE	MERGED TITLE/S
Family Circle	*Trio* (1964)
	Family (1964)
Good Housekeeping	*House Beautiful* (1968)
Harpers & Queen	*Queen* (1970)
	Harpers Bazaar (1970)
Mother	*Modern Mother* (1975)
Ideal Home	*In Store* (1987)
	Housewife (1968)
19	*Honey* (1986)
	Vanity Fair (1972)
	Woman & Beauty (1963)
Jackie	*Diana* (1976)
	Romeo (1974)
My Guy	*Oh Boy!* (1980)
	Mates (1981)
	Pink (1980)
	Fab (1980) (*Fab Hits, Fab 208*)
	O.K. (1977)

	Hi! (1976)
	Petticoat (1975)
	Trend (1976)
	Intro (1976)
	Boyfriend (1976)
Woman	*Woman's Mirror* (1966) (ex-*Woman's Sunday Mirror*)
	Woman's Illustrated (1961)
Woman & Home	*Good Life* (1980)
	My Home & Family (1971)
	Everywoman (1967)
	Modern Woman (1951)
	Modern Home (1951)
Woman's Journal	*Flair* (1972)
	Fashion (1969)
Woman's Own	*Woman's Day* (1961)
	Woman's Life (1934)
	Home Notes (1957)
Woman's Weekly	*Woman's Companion* (1961)
	Betty's Weekly (1916)
Homes & Gardens	*Home Magazine* (1963)
	Weldon's Ladies Journal (1954)
My Weekly	*Weekly Welcome* (1960)

Appendix II

Who owns What?

This is a list of some of the bigger magazine houses and their existing women's titles.

Argus Consumer Publications Ltd
12–18 Paul Street
London EC2A 4JS

Mother
Mother & Baby
Slimming
Successful Slimming
True Romance and True Story
Woman's Story

Argus Health Publications Ltd
30 Station Approach
West Byfleet
Surrey KT14 6NF

Green Cuisine
Here's Health

Benn Consumer Publications Ltd
Schweppes House
Grosvenor Road
St Albans
Herts AL1 3TN

Traditional Homes
Traditional Interior Decoration
Traditional Kitchens

Carlton Magazines
25 Newman Street
London W1P 3PE

Country Homes & Interiors
Look Now
Options
Woman's World
World of Interiors

Condé Nast Publications Ltd
Vogue House
Hanover Square
London W1R 0AD

Brides & Setting Up Home
House & Garden
The Tatler
Vogue
World of Interiors

D C Thomson & Co Ltd
Dundee
DD1 9QJ

Blue Jeans
Jackie
Patches
Annabel
Red Letter
Secrets
My Weekly
People's Friend

Emap Metro Publications Ltd
42–8 Gt Portland Street
London W1N 5AH

Just Seventeen
Looks
More!

G & J of the UK
Portland House
Stag Place
London SW1E 5AU

Prima
Best

International Publishing Corporation

IPC Holborn Group
Commonwealth House
1–19 New Oxford Street
London WC1A 1NG

Girl
Girl's Monthly
Mizz
My Guy
Photostory Monthlies
Loving Weekly
True Monthly

IPC Magazines Ltd
King's Reach Tower
Stamford Street
London SE1 9LS

Woman
Woman & Home
Woman's Own
Woman's Realm
Woman's Weekly
Essentials

IPC Women's Monthly Magazine Group
King's Reach Tower
Stamford Street
London SE1 9LS

Homes & Gardens
Ideal Home
Hair & Good Looks Book
19
Woman's Journal

The Business of Women's Magazines

International Thomson Publishing Ltd
38 Hans Crescent
London SW1X 0LZ

Family Circle
Living
Practical Parenting

National Magazine Co Ltd
National Magazine House
72 Broadwick Street
London W1V 2BP

Cosmopolitan
Company
Country Living
Good Housekeeping
Harpers & Queen
She

Appendix III

Biography

This is a biography of the main women's magazines in the post-Second World War period. They are magazines which were still extant after 1945 or have been launched since. The list includes magazines which have died since the war. The circulation quoted is the last published in the case of deceased titles (given in thousands) and the January–June 1987 ABC circulations in the case of existing magazines. Where the publication is not ABC or audited we state 'uncertified'. IPO means initial print order and free distribution is certified as VFD or BVS. Dead magazines we state 'no figures issued' if applicable.

To clarify the rather complicated IPC history, here are the relevant details:

- The Mirror Group bought Amalgamated Press in 1958 and renamed the company Fleetway Publications.
- Odhams Press bought Hulton Press and then George Newnes in 1959.
- The Mirror Group bought Odhams Press in 1961.
- IPC, as we know it today, was formed in 1968 and all departments moved to King's Reach Tower, Stamford Street, London SE1 9LS in 1976. There has been some movement out since, such as the Holborn Group.

Annabel

Owners:	D C Thomson & Co Ltd
	Dundee DD1 9QJ
Frequency:	Monthly
Launched:	1966
Circulation:	152,670

Baby – The Magazine

Owners:	Harrington Kilbride & Ptnrs Ltd
	21 Cross Street
	Islington
	London N1 2BH
Frequency:	Quarterly
Launched:	1978
Circulation:	Uncertified

Beauty & Skincare

Owners:	Beauty & Skincare Publishing
Frequency:	Twice yearly
Launched:	1980
Died:	1983
Circulation:	Unknown

Beauty Now – Over 21

Owners:	Spotlight Publications
	Greater London House
	Hampstead Road
	London NW1 7QZ
Frequency:	Thrice yearly
Launched:	1987
Circulation:	IPO 80,000

Bella

Owners:	Bauer (UK)
	The Publishing Consultancy
	15 Adeline Place
	London WC1B 3AJ
Frequency:	Weekly
Launched:	1987
Circulation:	IPO 1,000,000

Best

Owners:	G & J of the UK
	Portland House
	Stag Place
	London SW1E 5AU
Frequency:	Weekly
Launched:	1987
Circulation:	1,000,000 (est.)

Birmingham Woman
Owners: Timequart Ltd
               7–9 Euston Place
               Leamington Spa
               CV32 5LL
Frequency: Fortnightly
Launched: 1986
Circulation: Uncertified

Black Beauty & Hair
Owners: Hawker Consumer Publications Ltd
               13 Park House
               140 Battersea Park Road
               London SW11 4NB
Frequency: Quarterly
Launched: 1985
Circulation: 18,338 (Jan.–Dec. 1986)

Blue Jeans
Owners: D C Thomson & Co Ltd
               Dundee DD1 9QJ
Frequency: Weekly
Launched: 1977
Circulation: 108,182

Boyfriend
Owners: 1. City Magazines
               2. Fleetway
Frequency: Weekly
Launched: 1959
Died: 1966 (merged into **Trend**)
Circulation: 198,900

Brides & Setting Up Home
Owners: Condé Nast Publications Ltd
               Vogue House
               Hanover Square
               London W1R 0AD
Frequency: Six times a year
Launched: 1955
Circulation: 56,807

Britannia & Eve
Owners:	Illustrated Newspaper Group
Frequency:	Monthly
Launched:	1929 (having taken over Eve which was launched in 1919)
Died:	1957
Circulation:	No figures issued

Cachet
Owners:	Cachet Ltd
Frequency:	Monthly
Launched:	1985
Died:	1986
Circulation:	Uncertified

Candida
Owners	IPC Magazines Ltd
Frequency:	Weekly
Launched:	1972
Died:	1972
Circulation:	No figures issued

Capital Girl
Owners:	Gemini Publishing Ltd
Frequency:	Weekly
Launched:	1978
Died:	1978
Circulation:	No figures issued

Caroline
Owners:	British European Associated Publishers Ltd Glenthorne House Hammersmith Grove London W6 0LG
Frequency:	Monthly
Launched:	1987
Circulation:	Uncertified

Celebrity
Owners:	D C Thomson & Co Ltd Dundee DD1 9QJ
Frequency:	Weekly
Launched:	1986
Circulation:	128,950

Chat
Owners: Publishing Developments Ltd
             195 Knightsbridge
             London SW7 1RE
Frequency: Weekly
Launched: 1985
Circulation: 584,424

Chic Magazine
Owners: Ratepress Ltd
             94 Bow Road
             London E3 3AA
Frequency: Monthly
Launched: 1984
Circulation: Uncertified

Child's Play
Owners: Newbourne Group
             Greater London House
             Hampstead Road
             London NW1 7QQ
Frequency: Quarterly
Launched: 1987
Circulation: IPO 70,000

Company
Owners: National Magazine Co Ltd
             72 Broadwick Street
             London W1V 2BP
Frequency: Monthly
Launched: 1978
Circulation: 176,150

Cooks Weekly
Owners: 1. Marshall Cavendish
             2. Maxwell
             3. Northern & Shell
             4. GH Press Ltd
                Hemel Hempstead, Herts HP1 2RN
Frequency: Weekly
Launched: 1984
Circulation: Uncertified

Cosmopolitan

Owners: National Magazine Co Ltd
               72 Broadwick Street
               London W1V 2BP
Frequency: Monthly
Launched: 1972
Circulation: 375,894

Country Homes & Interiors

Owners: Carlton Magazines Ltd
               25 Newman Street
               London W1P 3PE
Frequency: Monthly
Launched: 1986
Circulation: 88,332

Country Living

Owners: National Magazine Co Ltd
               72 Broadwick Street
               London W1V 2BP
Frequency: Monthly
Launched: 1985
Circulation: 121,296

Date

Owners: Odhams Press
Frequency: Weekly
Launched: 1960
Died: 1961
Circulation: No figures issued

Diana

Owners: D C Thomson & Co Ltd
Frequency: Weekly
Launched: 1964
Died: 1976 (merged into **Jackie**)
Circulation: 139,220

Elle

Owners: News International Hachette Ltd
               PO Box 496
               Virginia Street
               London E1 9XT

Frequency: Monthly
Launched: 1985
Circulation: 239,605

Embroidery
Owners: E G Enterprises Ltd
               PO Box 428
               East Molesey
               Surrey KT8 9BB
Frequency: Quarterly
Launched: 1932
Circulation: Uncertified

Essentials
Owners: IPC Magazines Ltd
               King's Reach Tower
               Stamford Street
               London SE1 9LS
Frequency: Monthly
Launched: 1988
Circulation: IPO 750,000

Etcetra
Owners: D C Thomson & Co Ltd
Frequency: Fortnightly
Launched: 1985
Died: 1986
Circulation: Uncertified

Eve
Owners: Morgan Grampian Ltd
Frequency: Weekly
Launched: 1973
Died: 1973
Circulation: No figures issued

Everywoman
Owners: Everywoman Ltd
               34a Islington Green
               London N1 8DU
Frequency: Monthly
Launched: 1986
Circulation: Uncertified

Everywoman

Owners:	1. Odhams
	2. IPC Magazines Ltd
	King's Reach Tower
	Stamford Street
	London SE1 9LS
Frequency:	Monthly
Launched:	1934
Died:	1966 (merged into **Woman & Home**)
Circulation:	228,500

Exchange Contracts

Owners:	Home & Law Publishing Ltd
	Greater London House
	Hampstead Road
	London NW1 7QQ
Frequency:	Quarterly
Launched:	1979
Circulation:	248,719

Extra Special

Owners:	65 Blandford Street
	London W1H 3AJ
Frequency:	Bi-monthly
Launched:	1986
Circulation:	Uncertified

Fab Hits

Owners:	IPC Magazines Ltd
	King's Reach Tower
	Stamford Street
	London SE1 9LS
Frequency:	Weekly
Launched:	1964 as **Fab** (incorporating **Boyfriend** 1966, **Intro** 1976, **Trend** 1976, **Petticoat** 1975, **Hi!** 1976, **OK** 1977)
Died:	1980 (merged into **Oh Boy!**)
Circulation:	132,400

Faces

Owners:	Marshall Cavendish
Frequency:	Weekly
Launched:	1978
Died:	1978
Circulation:	No figures issued

Family
Owners: J Sainsbury Ltd
Frequency: Monthly
Launched: 1961
Died: 1964 (merged into **Family Circle**)
Circulation: No figures issued

Family Circle
Owners: International Thomson Publishing Ltd
                38 Hans Crescent
                London SW1X 0LZ
Frequency: Monthly
Launched: 1964
Circulation: 598,202

Fashion
Owners: Fleetway
Frequency: Monthly
Launched: 1968
Died: 1969 (merged into **Flair**)
Circulation: 88,450

Fashioncraft
Owners: Paterson Publications
Frequency: Bi-monthly
Launched: 1981
Died: 1984
Circulation: Uncertified

Fashion and Craft
Owners: Blenheim Publications Ltd
                1 Quebec Avenue
                Westerham
                Kent TN16 1BJ
Frequency: Quarterly
Launched: 1987
Circulation: Uncertified

Fashion Folio
Owners: IPC Women's Monthly Group
                King's Reach Tower
                Stamford Street
                London SE1 9LS
Frequency: Four times a year

Launched: 1987
Died: 1988 (merged into **Marie Claire**)
Circulation: Uncertified

Fenestra (Fashion – Sheffield)
Owners: Fenestra
                 1st Floor
                 Town Hall
                 High Street
                 Dronfield S18 6XN
Frequency: Fortnightly
Launched: 1982
Circulation: Uncertified

Fitness Magazine
Owners: 1. Stonehart Leisure
                 2. Northern & Shell plc
                    Northern & Shell Building
                    PO Box 381
                    Mill Harbour
                    London E14 9TW
Frequency: 13 issues a year
Launched: 1983
Circulation: 49,934

Fiz
Owners: Home & Law Magazine
Frequency: Four times a year
Launched: 1982
Died: 1985
Circulation: 405,000 (BVS)

Flair
Owners: 1. Newnes
                 2. IPC Magazines
Frequency: Monthly
Launched: 1960
Died: 1972 (incorporated into **Woman's Journal**)
Circulation: 82,733

Food Magazine
Owners: 1. Perry Publications
                 2. Trust House Forté

Frequency: Monthly
Launched: 1979 (incorporated **Freezer Family**)
Died: 1984
Circulation: Uncertified

Freezer Family
Owners: Freezer Family Ltd
Frequency: Monthly
Launched: 1972
Died: 1979 (incorporated into **Food Magazine**)
Circulation: No figures issued

Getting Married
Owners: Bounty Services Ltd
               140a Gloucester Mansions
               Cambridge Circus
               London WC2H 8HB
Frequency: Twice a year
Launched: 1987
Circulation: VFD 130,000

Girl
Owners: IPC Holborn Group
               Commonwealth House
               1–19 New Oxford Street
               London WC1A 1NG
Frequency: Weekly
Launched: 1986
Circulation: 105,285

Girl Monthly
Owners: IPC Holborn Group
               Commonwealth House
               1–19 New Oxford Street
               London WC1A 1NG
Frequency: Monthly
Launched: 1986
Circulation: 36,056

Girl About Town
Owners: Girl About Town Magazine Ltd
               Grosvenor House
               141–3 Drury Lane
               London WC2B 5TS

Frequency: Weekly
Launched: 1970
Circulation: 122,661

Glamour
Owners: Amalgamated Press
Launched: 1938
Died: 1956 (merged into **Mirabelle**; also contained
              Woman's Friend from 1950)
Circulation: No figures issued

Gloss Magazine
Owners: Gloss Ltd
              Baltic Chambers
              50 Wellington Street
              Glasgow G2 6HJ
Frequency: Ten times a year
Launched: 1985
Circulation: Uncertified

Going Shopping
Owners: CPR Publishing
              Northern Rock House
              20 Market Place
              Guisborough,
              Cleveland TS14 6HF
Frequency: Bi-monthly
Launched: 1985
Circulation: Uncertified

Good Housekeeping
Owners: National Magazine Co Ltd
              72 Broadwick Street
              London W1V 2BP
Frequency: Monthly
Launched: 1922
Circulation: 345,321

Good Life
Owners: IPC Magazines Ltd
Frequency: Monthly
Launched: 1978

Died: 1980 (merged into **Woman & Home**)
Circulation: 190,271

Green Cuisine
Owners: Argus Health Publications Ltd
                 30 Station Approach
                 West Byfleet
                 Surrey KT14 6NF
Frequency: Quarterly
Launched: 1986
Circulation: Uncertified

Guiding (formerly **Guider**)
Owners: Girl Guides Association
                 17–19 Buckingham Palace Road
                 London SW1W 0PT
Frequency: Monthly
Launched: 1913
Circulation: Uncertified

Hair
Owners: Reed Business Publishing Ltd
                 Quadrant House
                 The Quadrant
                 Sutton,
                 Surrey SM2 5AS
Frequency: Four times a year
Launched: 1977
Circulation: 208,269

Hair & Good Looks Book
Owners: IPC Women's Monthly Magazine Group
                 King's Reach Tower
                 Stamford Street
                 London SE1 9LS
Frequency: Bi-monthly
Launched: 1984
Circulation: 121,141

Hair Care
Owners: Atlas Publishing Co Ltd
                 334 Brixton Road
                 London SW9 7AG

Frequency: Bi-monthly
Launched: 1982
Circulation: Uncertified

Hair Flair
Owners: 1. HairFlair Ltd
        2. Redwood Publishing (Consumer) Ltd
           20–26 Brunswick Place
           London N1 6DJ
Frequency: Monthly
Launched: 1982
Circulation: 44,498

Hair Now – Over 21
Owners: Spotlight Publications
        Greater London House
        Hampstead Road
        London NW1 7QZ
Frequency: Quarterly
Launched: 1986
Circulation: Uncertified

Harpers Bazaar
Owners: National Magazine Co Ltd
Frequency: Monthly
Launched: 1929
Died: 1970 (merged with **Queen** into **Harpers & Queen**)
Circulation: 43,046

Harpers & Queen
Owners: National Magazine Co Ltd
        72 Broadwick Street
        London W1V 2BP
Frequency: Monthly
Launched: **Harper's Bazaar** 1929
        The Queen 1861
        Harpers & Queen 1970
Circulation: 98,904

Heartbeat
Owners: IPC Magazines Ltd
Frequency: Weekly
Launched: 1981

Died: 1982
Circulation: Uncertified

Here's Health
Owners: 1. Newman Turner Publications
               2. Argus Health Publications Ltd
                  30 Station Approach
                  West Byfleet
                  Surrey KT14 6NF
Frequency: Monthly
Launched: 1956
Circulation: 55,959

Hers
Owners: 1. Pearsons
               2. IPC Magazines Ltd
Frequency: Monthly
Launched: 1966 (incorporating New Love 1977)
Died: 1984
Circulation: 85,000

Hi!
Owners: IPC Magazines Ltd
Frequency: Weekly
Launched: 1975
Died: 1976 (merged into OK)
Circulation: 103,176

Home & Country
Owners: National Federation of Women's Institutes
               39 Eccleston Street
               London SW1 9NT
Frequency: Monthly
Launched: 1919
Circulation: 102,715

Home Chat
Owners: Amalgamated Press
Frequency: Weekly
Launched: 1895
Died: 1958
Circulation: 127,500

Home Companion
Owners: Newnes
Frequency: Weekly
Launched: 1897
Died: 1956
Circulation: No figures issued

Home and Family
Owners: The Mothers' Union
               181 Queen Victoria Street
               London EC4V 4DD
Frequency: Monthly
Launched: 1888
Circulation: Uncertified

Home & Freezer Digest
Owners: British European Associated Publishers
               Glenthorne House
               Hammersmith Grove
               London W6 0LG
Frequency: Monthly
Launched: 1975
Circulation: 204,083

Home Improvements Guides (formerly **Home Improvements**)
Owners: Property Books Ltd
               248 High Street
               Croydon, Surrey CR0 1NF
Frequency: Six times a year
Launched: 1979
Circulation: 29,481

Homes & Gardens
Owners: 1. Newnes
               2. IPC Women's Monthly Magazines Group
                  King's Reach Tower
                  Stamford Street
                  London SE1 9LS
Frequency: Monthly
Launched: 1919
Circulation: 198,188

184

Home Notes
Owners: Newnes
Frequency: Weekly
Launched: 1894
Died: 1957 (merged into **Woman's Own**)
Circulation: 238,300

Honey
Owners: IPC Magazines Ltd
               King's Reach Tower
               Stamford Street
               London SE1 9LS
Frequency: Monthly
Launched: 1960
Died: 1986 (merged into **19**)
Circulation: 118,000

House Beautiful
Owners: National Magazine Co Ltd
Frequency: Monthly
Launched: 1954
Died: 1968 (merged into **Good Housekeeping**)
Circulation: 50,000

House & Garden (incorporating **Wine & Food Magazine**)
Owners: Condé Nast Publications Ltd
               Vogue House
               Hanover Square
               London W1R 0AD
Frequency: Monthly
Launched: 1947
Circulation: 137,022

Housewife
Owners: 1. Hulton Press
               2. Odhams
Frequency: Monthly
Launched: 1939
Died: 1967 (merged into **Ideal Home**)
Circulation: 136,000

Ideal Home
Owners: 1. Odhams
               2. IPC Women's Monthly Magazines Group

King's Reach Tower
Stamford Street
London SE1 9LS

Frequency:	Monthly
Launched:	1920
Circulation:	242,471

Image
Owners:	Image Publications Ltd
	22 Crofton Road
	Dun Laoghaire
	Co. Dublin
Frequency:	Monthly
Circulation:	Uncertified

Inhabit
Owners:	Link House
Frequency:	Monthly
Launched:	1973
Died:	1974
Circulation:	No figures issued

Intro
Owners:	Odhams Press Ltd
Frequency:	Weekly
Launched:	1967
Died:	1967
Circulation:	No figures issued

In Store
Owners:	IPC Magazines Ltd
Frequency:	Monthly
Launched:	1985
Died:	1987 (merged into **Ideal Home**)
Circulation:	107,000

IT Magazine (Irish Tatler)
Owners:	The Village Centre
	Ballybrack Village
	Co Dublin
Frequency:	Monthly
Launched:	1890
Circulation:	Uncertified

Jackie
Owners: D C Thomson & Co Ltd
               Dundee DD1 9QJ
Frequency: Weekly
Launched: 1963
Circulation: 222,356

Just Seventeen
Owners: Emap Metro Publications Ltd
               52–55 Carnaby Street
               London W1.
Frequency: Weekly
Launched: 1983
Circulation: 278,039

Keep Fit Magazine
Owners: Second City Advtg & Publishing Ltd
               Albany House
               Hurst Street
               Birmingham B5 4BB
Frequency: Monthly
Launched: 1987
Circulation: Uncertified

Kitchen Choice
Owners: Oberon Publishing
Frequency: Monthly
Launched: 1984
Died: 1985
Circulation: Uncertified

Knit & Stitch
Owners: Ingrid Publishing Ltd
               Pinewood Studios
               Iver Heath
               Bucks SL0 0NH
Frequency: Monthly
Launched: 1985
Circulation: Uncertified

The Lady
Owners: The Lady
               39–40 Bedford Street
               London WC2E 9ER

Frequency: Weekly
Launched: 1885
Circulation: 65,581

Lady Gossip
Owners: Fabie Creative Images
              1 Clarendon Avenue
              Altrincham
              Cheshire WA15 8HD
Frequency: Monthly
Launched: 1983
Circulation: Uncertified

Lipstick
Owners: Tala Publications plc
Frequency: Monthly
Launched: 1985
Circulation: Uncertified

Living
Owners: International Thomson Publishing Ltd
              38 Hans Crescent
              London SW1X 0LZ
Frequency: Monthly
Launched: 1967
Circulation: 331,356

Looking Good
Owners: Penny Vincenzi Publications Ltd
Frequency: Monthly
Launched: 1972
Died: 1973
Circulation: No figures issued

Look Now
Owners: Carlton Magazines Ltd
              25 Newman Street
              London W1P 3PE
Frequency: Monthly
Launched: 1972
Circulation: 99,455

Looks
Owners: Emap Metro Publications Ltd
42–48 Great Portland Street
London W1N 5AH
Frequency: Monthly
Launched: 1985
Circulation: 147,429

Love Affair
Owners: IPC Magazines Ltd
Frequency: Weekly
Launched: 1970
Died: 1982 (merged into **Loving**)
Circulation: 99,000

Loving Weekly (formerly Loving)
Owners: IPC Magazines Ltd
King's Reach Tower
Stamford Street
London SE1 9LS
Frequency: Weekly
Launched: 1970
Circulation: 75,037

Machine Knitting News
Owners: Litharne Ltd
PO Box 9
Stratford-upon-Avon
Warwickshire CV37 8RS
Frequency: Monthly
Launched: 1984
Circulation: 47,492

Machine Knitting World
Owners: 1/2 East Market Street
Newport
Gwent NP9 2AY
Frequency: Bi-monthly
Launched: 1984
Circulation: Uncertified

Majesty
Owners: Hanover Magazines Ltd

                        80 Highgate Road
                        London NW5 1PB
Frequency: Monthly
Launched: 1983
Circulation: 69,178

Marilyn
Owners: Amalgamated Press Ltd
Frequency: Weekly
Launched: 1957
Died: 1965
Circulation: 115,700

Marty
Owners: Newnes
Frequency: Weekly
Launched: 1959
Died: 1963
Circulation: 159,000

Maternity and Mothercraft
Owners: Newbourne Group Ltd
                        Greater London House
                        Hampstead Road
                        London NW1 7QQ
Frequency: Bi-monthly
Launched: 1967
Circulation: Uncertified

Mates
Owners: IPC Magazines Ltd
Frequency: Weekly
Launched: 1975
Died: 1981 (merged into **Oh Boy!**)
Circulation: 104,000

Mayfair
Owners: Spry Publications Ltd
Frequency: Monthly
Launched: 1946
Died: 1950
Circulation: No figures issued

Mirabelle
Owners: 1. Amalgamated Press Ltd
                 2. IPC Magazines Ltd
Frequency: Monthly
Launched: 1956
Died: 1977 (merged into **Pink**. Also included *3lamour* which
                 was merged into **Mirabelle** in 1956. **Glamour** contained
                 Woman's Friend which was merged into it in 1950)
Circulation: 74,355

Mizz
Owners: IPC Holborn Group
                 Commonwealth House
                 1–19 New Oxford Street
                 London WC1A 1NG
Frequency: Fortnightly
Launched: 1985
Circulation: 133,959

Ms London Weekly
Owners: Employment Publications Ltd
                 7/9 Rathbone Street
                 London W1P 1AF
Frequency: Weekly
Launched: 1968
Circulation: 136,355

M & S Magazine
Owners: Redwood Publishing
                 141–3 Drury Lane
                 London WC2B 5TF
Frequency: Quarterly
Launched: 1987
Circulation: IPO 1,300,000

Modern Woman
Owners: Newnes
Frequency: Monthly
Launched: 1925 (included **Modern Home** 1928–51)
Died: 1965
Circulation: 134,400

More!
Owners: Emap Metro Magazines Ltd
               42–48 Great Portland Street
               London W1.
Frequency: Monthly
Launched: 1988
Circulation: IPO 225,000

Mother (incorporating **Modern Mother**)
Owners: 1. IPC Magazines Ltd
               2. Argus Consumer Publications Ltd
                  12–18 Paul Street
                  London EC2A 4JS
Frequency: Monthly
Launched: 1936
Circulation: 74,005

Mother & Baby
Owners: Argus Consumer Publications Ltd
               12–18 Paul Street
               London EC2A 4JS
Frequency: Monthly
Launched: 1956
Circulation: 110,091

Mother and Child
Owners: Bounty Vision Ltd
               140A Gloucester Mansions
               Cambridge Street
               London WC2H 8HD
Frequency: Twice yearly
Launched: 1983
Circulation: Uncertified

My Guy
Owners: IPC Holborn Group
               Commonwealth House
               1–19 New Oxford Street
               London WC1A 1NG
Frequency: Weekly
Launched: 1978
Circulation: 82,975

My Home & Family
Owners: Fleetway
Frequency: Monthly
Launched: Contained **My Home** (1928) and **Wife & Home** (1929)
Died: 1971 (merged into **Woman & Home**)
Circulation: 101,380

My Story
Owners: My Story
                 PO Box 94
                 London W4 2ER
Frequency: Monthly
Launched: 1964
Circulation: No figures issued

My Weekly
Owners: D C Thomson & Co Ltd
                 Dundee DD1 9QJ
Frequency: Weekly
Launched: 1910
Circulation: 607,065

New Homemaker (previously **Homemaker**)
Owners: IPC Magazines Ltd
Frequency: Monthly
Launched: 1980 (**Homemaker** launched 1969)
Died: 1981 (merged into **Practical Householder**)
Circulation: Uncertified

New Woman
Publishers: Murdoch Magazines
                 PO Box 496
                 Virginia Street
                 London E1 9XT
Frequency: Monthly
Launched: 1988
Circulation: IPO 400,000

New Warwickshire Woman
Owners: New Warwickshire Woman
                 30 Hamilton Terrace
                 Royal Leamington Spa
                 CV32 4LY

Frequency: Bi-monthly
Launched: 1985
Circulation: Uncertified

19
Owners: IPC Women's Monthly Magazines Group
                King's Reach Tower
                Stamford Street
                London SE1 9LS
Frequency: Monthly
Launched: 1968
Circulation: 136,660

Nouvelle
Owners: Joint Marketing & Services Ltd
Frequency: Quarterly
Launched: 1985
Died: 1985
Circulation: Uncertified

Nova
Owners: 1. Newnes
                2. IPC Magazines Ltd
Frequency: Monthly
Launched: 1965
Died: 1975
Circulation: 86,000

Nursery World
Owners: Bouverie Publishing Co Ltd
                Cliffords Inn
                Fetter Lane, Fleet Street
                London EC4A 1PJ
Frequency: Fortnightly
Launched: 1925
Circulation: No figures issued

Office Secretary
Owners: Trade Media Ltd
                Streetfield House
                Carterton
                Oxford OX8 3XZ
Frequency: Quarterly

Launched: 1987
Circulation: Uncertified

Oh Boy!
Owners: IPC Magazines
Frequency: Weekly
Launched: 1976
Died: 1985 (merged into **My Guy**)
Circulation: 100,000

OK
Owners: IPC Magazines Ltd
Frequency: Weekly
Launched: 1975
Died: 1977 (merged into **Fab 208**)
Circulation: 82,533

Options
Owners: Carlton Magazines
              25 Newman Street
              London W1P 3PE
Frequency: Monthly
Launched: 1982
Circulation: 236,117

Over 21
Owners: 1. MS Publishing Ltd
              2. Spotlight Publications
                 Greater London House
                 Hampstead Road
                 London NW1 7QZ
Frequency: Monthly
Launched: 1972
Circulation: 86,624

Parent Care
Owners: 1. Pearl Assurance Marketing Service Ltd
              2. The Newbourne Group
                 Greater London House
                 Hampstead Road
                 London NW1 7QQ
Frequency: Quarterly
Launched: 1986
Circulation: Uncertified

Parents
Owners: Gemini Magazines Ltd
                Victory House
                Leicester Place
                London WC2 7NB
Frequency: Monthly
Launched: 1976
Circulation: 93,801

Patches
Owners: D C Thomson & Co Ltd
                Dundee DD1 9QJ
Frequency: Weekly
Launched: 1979
Circulation: 74,102

People's Friend
Owners: D C Thomson & Co Ltd
                Dundee DD1 9QJ
Frequency: Weekly
Launched: 1869
Circulation: 595,567

Personal
Owners: Carlton Publishing
Frequency: Monthly
Launched: 1974
Died: 1975
Circulation: No figures issued

Pins and Needles
Owners: 1. International Thomson
                2. Consumer & Industrial Press Ltd
                   Milford House
                   6–10 Kirby Street
                   London EC1N 8TS
Frequency: Monthly
Launched: 1949
Circulation: 32,965

Petticoat
Owners: Fleetway
Frequency: Weekly

Launched: 1966
Died: 1975 (merged with **Hi!**)
Circulation: 151,985

Photolove
Owners: IPC Magazines
Frequency: Weekly
Died: 1983 (merged into **Secrets**)
Circulation: 122,000

Photo Secret Love
Owners: IPC Magazines
Frequency: Weekly
Launched: 1981
Died: 1982 (merged into **Secret Love**)
Circulation: Uncertified

Photostory Monthlies
Owners: IPC Holborn Group
              Commonwelath House
              1–19 New Oxford Street
              London WC1A 1NG
Frequency: Monthlies
              Five magazines: **Photolove Monthly, My Guy Monthly,
              Oh Boy Monthly, True Monthly, Girl Monthly**
Circulation: Combined 180,407

Pink
Owners: IPC Magazines
Frequency: Weekly
Launched: 1973
Died: 1980 (merged into **Mates**)
Circulation: 124,750

Practical Parenting
Owners: International Thomson Publishing Ltd
              38 Hans Crescent
              London SW1X 0LZ
Frequency: Monthly
Launched: 1988
Circulation: No figures issued

Prima

Owners:	BSR (Publications) Ltd
Frequency:	Monthly
Launched:	1976
Died:	1977
Circulation:	No figures issued

Prima

Owners:	G & J of the UK
	Portland House
	Stag Place
	London SW1E 5AU
Frequency:	Monthly
Launched:	1986
Circulation:	993,018

Queen

Owners:	1. Several
	2. Stevens Press Ltd 1957
	3. Oxley Press Ltd 1968
	4. National Magazine Co Ltd
Frequency:	Fortnightly
Launched:	1861
Died:	1970 (merged with **Harper's Bazaar** into **Harpers & Queen**)
Circulation:	40,026

Red Letter

Owners:	D C Thomson & Co Ltd
	Dundee DD1 9QJ
Frequency:	Weekly
Launched:	1899
Circulation:	23,208

Red Star Weekly

Owners:	D C Thomson & Co Ltd
	Dundee DD1 9QJ
Frequency:	Weekly
Launched:	1929
Died:	1983
Circulation:	31,000

Rio
Owners: Link House
Frequency: Monthly
Launched: 1981
Died: 1982 (merged into IPC's Hers)
Circulation: Uncertified

Riva
Owners: Carlton Magazines
                 25 Newman Street
                 London W1P 3PE
Frequency: Weekly
Launched: 1988
Circulation: IPO 350,000

Romance
Owners: Romance Magazine
                 PO Box 94
                 London W4 2ER
Frequency: Monthly
Launched: 1969
Circulation: No figures issued

Romany
Owners: Petulengro Magazines
Frequency: Monthly
Launched: 1983
Died: 1985
Circulation: Uncertified

Romeo
Owners: D C Thomson & Co Ltd
Frequency: Weekly
Launched: 1957
Died: 1974 (merged into **Diana**)
Circulation: 91,577

Roxy
Owners: Amalgamated Press Ltd
Frequency: Weekly
Launched: 1957
Died: 1963
Circulation: 115,743

Secrets
Owners:	D C Thomson & Co Ltd
	Dundee DD1 9QJ
Frequency:	Weekly
Launched:	1932
Circulation:	27,572

Sew Into Fashion With Betty Foster
Owners:	Litharne Ltd
	PO Box 9
	Stratford-upon-Avon
Frequency:	Four times a year
Launched:	1985
Circulation:	Uncertified

She
Owners:	National Magazine Co Ltd
	72 Broadwick Street
	London W1V 2BP
Frequency:	Monthly
Launched:	1955
Circulation:	212,115

Sheba Magazine
Owners:	Sheba Publications Ltd
Frequency:	Monthly
Launched:	1979
Died:	1980
Circulation:	30,000 (PO)

Shopping Scene
Owners:	Purnell & Sons Ltd
Frequency:	Twice a year
Launched:	1959
Died:	1983
Circulation:	Ten million (hand distribution)

Simplicity Magazine
Owners:	Style Patterns Ltd
	35/39 South Ealing Road
	London W5 4QT
Frequency:	Three times a year
Launched:	1964
Circulation:	41,654

Sincerely
Owners: Newnes
Frequency: Monthly
Launched: 1858
Died: 1961 (merged into True)
Circulation: 79,037

Slimmer
Owners: Slimmer Publications Ltd
               The Grove
               Pipers Lane
               Harpenden, Herts AL5 1AH
Frequency: Bi-monthly
Launched: 1975
Circulation: 140,058

Slimming
Owners: Slimming Magazine (Argus Press)
               Victory House
               Leicester Place
               London WC2H 7QP
Frequency: Six times a year
Launched: 1969
Circulation: 241,238

Slimming Naturally
Owners: Newman Turner Publications Ltd
Frequency: Six times a year
Launched: 1978
Died: 1980
Circulation: 73,000

Spare Rib
Owners: Spare Rib Ltd
               27 Clerkenwell Close
               London EC1R 0AT
Frequency: Monthly
Launched: 1972
Circulation: No figures issued

Stitchcraft
Owners: Stitchcraft Ltd
Frequency: Monthly
Launched: 1932

Died: 1982
Circulation: 55,000

Style Magazine
Owners: Style Patterns Ltd
               35–39 South Ealing Road
               London W5 4QT
Frequency: Three times a year
Launched: 1969
Circulation: 44,525

Successful Slimming
Owners: 1. IPC Magazines Ltd
               2. Argus Consumer Publications Ltd
                  12–18 Paul Street
                  London EC2 4JS
Frequency: Bi-monthly
Launched: 1976
Circulation: 93,921

Superstore
Owners: Home & Law Magazines
Frequency: Four times a year
Launched: 1981
Died: 1985
Circulation: Uncertified

Taste
Owners: 1. Marshall Cavendish
               2. British European Associated Publishers Ltd
                  Glenthorne House
                  Hammersmith Grove
                  London W6 0LG
Frequency: Monthly
Launched: 1986
Circulation: 56,141

The Tatler
Owners: 1. Illustrated Newspapers Ltd
               2. Thomsons
               3. Country Illustrated Magazine Group
               4. Tatler & Bystander Publishing Ltd
               5. Tatler Publishing Co Ltd (Condé Nast)

Vogue House
Hanover Square
London W1R 0AD

Frequency: Monthly
Launched: 1709 (died 1966, relaunched briefly as **London
              Life**, resurrected in 1968 as **The Tatler**)
Circulation: 60,845

Tomorrow

Owners: Katherine Hamnett
Frequency: Bi-monthly
Launched: 1985
Died: 1985
Circulation: Uncertified

The Townswoman

Owners: The National Union of Townswomen's Guilds
              2 Cromwell Place
              South Kensington
              London SW7 2JG
Frequency: Monthly (except August)
Launched: 1933
Circulation: 39,906

Traditional Homes

Owners: 1. CFE Publishing
              2. Benn Consumer Periodicals Ltd
                 Schweppes House
                 Grosvenor Road
                 St Albans
                 Herts AL1 3TN
Frequency: Monthly
Launched: 1984
Circulation: Uncertified

Traditional Interior Decoration

Owners: Benn Consumer Periodicals Ltd
              Schweppes House
              Grosvenor Road
              St Albans
              Herts AL1 3TN
Frequency: Alternate months
Launched: 1987
Circulation: Uncertified

Traditional Kitchens Magazines
Owners: Benn Consumer Periodicals Ltd
                  Schweppes House
                  Grosvenor Road
                  St Albans
                  Herts AL1 3TN
Frequency: Alternate months
Launched: 1986
Circulation: Uncertified

Trend
Owners: City Magazines Ltd
Frequency: Weekly
Launched: 1966
Died: 1967 (merged into **Petticoat**)
Circulation: 146,901

True
Owners: IPC Magazines Ltd
Frequency: Monthly
Launched: 1944
Died: 1984
Circulation: Uncertified

True Monthly
Owners: IPC Holborn Group
                  Commonwealth House
                  1–19 New Oxford Street
                  London WC1A 1NG
Frequency: Monthly
Launched: 1987
Circulation: IPO 80,000

True Romances
Owners: Argus Consumer Publications Ltd
                  12–18 Paul Street
                  London EC2A 4JS
Frequency: Monthly
Launched: 1934
Circulation: 167,784 (combined with **True Story**)

True Story
Owners: Argus Consumer Publications Ltd

12–18 Paul Street
London EC2A 4JS

Frequency:	Monthly
Launched:	1922
Circulation:	167,784 (combined with **True Romances**)

Valentine

Owners:	Fleetway
Frequency:	Weekly
Launched:	1957
Died:	1974
Circulation:	100,517

Vanity Fair

Owners:	1. The National Magazine Co Ltd
	2. IPC Magazines Ltd
	King's Reach Tower
	Stamford Street
	London SE1 9LS
Frequency:	Monthly
Launched:	1949
Died:	1972 (sold to IPC and merged into **Honey**)
Circulation:	93,380

Viva

Owners:	Penthouse Publications
Frequency:	Monthly
Launched:	1974
Died:	1979
Circulation:	No figures issued

Vogue

Owners:	Condé Nast Publications Ltd
	Vogue House
	Hanover Square
	London W1R 0AD
Frequency:	Monthly
Launched:	1916
Circulation:	180,836

Vogue Patterns

Owners:	Butterick Company Ltd
	New Lane

Havant
Hants PO29 2ND

Frequency: Six times a year
Launched: 1934
Circulation: 74,233

W
Owners: Queensway Publishing
Frequency: Fortnightly
Launched: 1987
Circulation: IPO 49,000

Wedding and Home (formerly Wedding Day and First Home)
Owners: 1. Socio Magazines Ltd
               2. Home & Law (Wedding Publications) Ltd
                  Greater London House
                  Hampstead Road
                  London NW1 7QP
Frequency: Six times a year
Launched: 1975
Circulation: 38,283

Weight Watchers
Owners: Weight Watchers
               Fairacres Estate
               Dedworth Road
               Windsor, Berks SL4 4UY
Frequency: Six times a year
Launched: 1977
Circulation: 96,631

Weldon's Ladies Journal
Owners: Amalgamated Press
Frequency: Weekly
Launched: 1879
Died: 1954 (merged into Home, which was
               merged into Homes & Gardens 1963)
Circulation: No figures issued

Wessex Woman
Owners: Dorchester Publications Ltd
               128 Old Winton Road
               Andover, Hampshire

Frequency: Bi-monthly
Launched: 1987
Circulation: IPO 25,000

What Diet & Lifestyle
Owners: AIM Publications Ltd
              Silver House
              31–5 Beak Street
              London W1R 3LD
Frequency: Bi-monthly
Launched: 1983
Circulation: 41,695

Woman
Owners: 1. Odhams
              2. IPC Magazines Ltd
                 King's Reach Tower
                 Stamford Street
                 London SE1 9LS
Frequency: Weekly
Launched: 1937
Circulation: 1,061,967

Woman & Beauty
Owners: Newnes
Frequency: Monthly
Launched: 1930
Died: 1963
Circulation: 73,700

Woman Bride and Home
Owners: 1. Odhams
              2. IPC Magazines Ltd
                 King's Reach Tower
                 Stamford Street
                 London SE1 9LS
Frequency: Six times a year
Launched: 1968
Died: 1972
Circulation: 72,416

Womancraft with Sewing and Knitting
Owners: 1. Astra Press Ltd 1972

                    2. The National Magazine Co Ltd 1974
                    3. IPC Magazines Ltd
                    4. Paterson Publications
Frequency: Monthly (merged **Womancraft** with **Sewing and Knitting**
                    by IPC in 1977)
Died: 1982
Circulation: 65,800

Woman and Home
Owners: 1. Amalgamated Press (Fleetway)
                    2. IPC Magazines Ltd
                       King's Reach Tower
                       Stamford Street
                       London SE1 9LS
Frequency: Monthly
Launched: 1926
Circulation: 587,909

Woman's Choice
Owners: Creation Ltd
Frequency: Weekly
Launched: 1974
Died: 1974
Circulation: No figures issued

Woman's Companion
Owners: Amalgamated Press
Frequency: Weekly
Launched: 1927
Died: 1961 (merged into **Woman's Weekly**)
Circulation: 177,500

Woman's Day
Owners: Newnes
Frequency: Weekly
Launched: 1958
Died: 1961 (merged into **Woman's Own**)
Circulation: 888,500

Woman's Friend
Owners: Pearsons (Newnes)
Frequency: Weekly
Launched: 1924

Died: 1950 (merged into **Glamour**)
Circulation: 199,008

Woman's Illustrated
Owners: Odhams
Frequency: Weekly
Launched: 1936
Died: 1961 (merged into **Woman**)
Circulation: 676,800

Woman's Journal
Owners: 1. Fleetway
             2. IPC Magazines Ltd
                King's Reach Tower
                Stamford Street
                London SE1 9LS
Frequency: Monthly
Launched: 1927
Circulation: 230,320

Woman's Mirror
Owners: 1. Fleetway
             2. IPC Magazines Ltd
Frequency: Weekly (was formerly **Woman's Sunday Mirror**,
             national newspaper for women launched in 1955)
Launched: 1958
Died: 1967 (merged into **Woman**)
Circulation: 858,600

Woman's Own
Owners: 1. Newnes
             2. IPC Magazines Ltd
                King's Reach Tower
                Stamford Street
                London SE1 9LS
Frequency: Weekly
Launched: 1932
Circulation: 1,113,080

Woman's Realm
Owners: 1. Odhams
             2. IPC Magazines Ltd
                King's Reach Tower

<pre>
                        Stamford Street
                        London SE1 9LS
Frequency: Weekly
Launched: 1958
Circulation: 625,469
</pre>

Woman's Story

<pre>
Owners: Argus Consumer Publications Ltd
              12–18 Paul Street
              London EC2A 4JS
Frequency: Monthly
Launched: 1956
Circulation: 60,205
</pre>

Woman's Way

<pre>
Owners: J S Publications Ltd
              126 Lower Baggot Street
              Dublin 2
Frequency: Weekly
Launched: 1978
Circulation: 70,101
</pre>

Woman's Weekly

<pre>
Owners: 1. Fleetway
              2. IPC Magazines Ltd
                 King's Reach Tower
                 Stamford Street
                 London SE1 9LS
Frequency: Weekly
Launched: 1911
Circulation: 1,325,742
</pre>

Woman's World

<pre>
Owners: Carlton Magazines Ltd
              25 Newman Street
              London W1P 3HA
Frequency: Monthly
Launched: 1977
Circulation: 214,276
</pre>

Woman's World

<pre>
Owners: Odhams
Frequency: Weekly
</pre>

Launched: 1903
Died: 1958
Circulation: 100,900

Women's Review
Owners: Women's Review Ltd
              Old Loom House
              Back Church Lane
              London E1 1LS
Frequency: Monthly
Launched: **1987**
Circulation: Uncertified

Working Woman
Owners: 1. Wintour Publications
              2. Peter Cadbury
              3. Preston Publications
Frequency: Monthly
Launched: 1984
Died: 1987
Circulation: Uncertified

World of Knitting
Owners: 1/2 East Market Street
              Newport, Gwent
Frequency: Monthly
Launched: 1983
Circulation: 28,982

Young Mother
Owners: Family Publications Ltd
              24–25 Cowcross Street
              London EC1M 6DQ
Frequency: Bi-monthly
Launched: (Relaunched 1987)
Circulation: IPO 90,000

Your Baby
Owners: Cirrus Publishing
Frequency: Monthly
Launched: 1985
Died: 1985
Circulation: Uncertified

The Business of Women's Magazines

Your Hair

Owners:	Half Acre
	Lankhurst Oak
	Blackboys
	Uckfield, Sussex
Frequency:	Monthly
Launched:	1985
Circulation:	Uncertified

Index

Index

Index

Index